A Passion for Poetry

A Collection of Poems

By
Sandra Cairine MacLeod

authorHOUSE®

AuthorHouse™
1663 Liberty Drive
Bloomington, IN 47403
www.authorhouse.com
Phone: 1-800-839-8640

First published by AuthorHouse   3/30/2010

ISBN: 978-1-4520-0327-6 (sc)

Printed in the United States of America
Bloomington, Indiana

This book is printed on acid-free paper.

Acknowledgments

*I thank those
who've
walked with me
along this
path of mine,
sharing time
and wisdom
with thoughts
of the
Divine.*

*I thank all
family members
and of course
my treasured friends,
because they've
enhanced
my journey
with the time
that they
do spend.*

*I thank all new
acquaintance
for their input
and their drive,
they make
my life
much richer
as do those
who pass
me by.*

Thank You, Thank you, Thank you...

Dedication

This book is dedicated with love to my parents
Gordon and Diana MacLeod
who have since passed
to the other side.
Treasured are their memories
and the messages received.

Until we meet again...

Contents

A Blessing

Grandchildren are a blessing
the sweetness of the earth,
embracing joy and happiness
from the moment of their birth.
Enjoy your 'Little Angels'
as they grow so very fast,
absorb them with each breath you take
'sweet memories to last'.
They fill your arms with wonder,
they fill your hearts with love,
they fill your life with living,
they're a blessing from above.
The years pass by so quickly,
their firsts are all but gone,
for time, it waits for no-one,
'life is like a marathon'.
These 'Little Angels' grow so fast
their cuddles cease to be,
for shyness takes them over
when there are others who can see.
It isn't cool, don't you know
to show affection, love or pride,
cheeks grow red, they bow their heads
desperately trying to hide.
But when alone in the comforts of home,
cuddles come free of charge,
as you soak it up and fill your cup
your spirit will boost and recharge.
Yes, Grandchildren are a blessing,
our future as we're present and past,
with bonds made strong while living
family ties go unsurpassed.

A Place in Mind

Way out of town through the hills, grass and trees,
the birds singing gaily in the soft summer breeze.
A small little cabin with just enough room,
a lake right beside it, the flowers in bloom.
The kitchen is warmed by a wood stove you see,
and on the shelves by the windows, growing spices there'd be.
A fireplace built out of rocks that I chose,
with a chair right beside it to warm fingers and toes.
A couch and a love seat, a chair with a stool,
a wooden chest for the logs that I'd use for my fuel.
The tables are old but re-done to perfection,
the beauty of their being would hold my affection.
Two bedrooms on the main floor cozy yet small,
a big bathroom with cupboards right down the hall.
On the windows, crochet curtains would hang for some shade,
and on the tables and dressers matching doilies there laid.
Hand braided rugs and pillows with feathers,
a basin and jug, all old fashioned treasures.
The stairway's hand carved with roses and vines,
and like those on the windows, polished to shine.
A loft up on top with a window up high,
so at night I could see all the stars in the sky.
This is only a dream, a place in my mind,
but when lost in my thoughts - it's so easy to find.

Advertising

Methods to gain attention surround us every day,
in magazines and handbills - Ads are much displayed.
In the mail and the paper more flyers do appear,
when riding public transit messages are also clear.

Billboards flash right past us as the Image stays in mind,
television and the radio repeat the main Headline.
We listen, look and read as interest is inspired,
Illustrations and the Copy create need and sweet desire.

The Signature or Symbol are retained for future use,
when next you visit the market or are let out on the loose
Four types of Advertisements show items worldwide,
Repetitive reminds us of a brand that's true and tried.

Informational breed's intelligence and at times some guarantees,
Testimonial draws the impact of famed personalities.
Emotional involves the feelings of joy and fear and pride,
human nature at it's finest doesn't like to be denied.

Advertising is a Science that's been used for many years,
with displays for every season creating atmospheres.
There is a special recipe to enhance success of sales,
it's called the AIDA Formula and it's used to tip the scales.

Attention, Interest and Desire shift Action into gear,
and then we seem to find ourselves across from the cashier.
We're caught up in a system that reads us like a book,
and much like fish in water - at some point we've been hooked.

All We Need

Life and love and happiness
are enhanced by who we know,
each treasure that we find on earth
has a special glow.
Friendships we are blessed with
family strong and true,
are all we really need in life
to help us make it through.

Careers that feed ambitions
creative juices flowing free,
co-workers to converse with
as employer or employee.
Interests with a place to grow
Mother Nature's inspiring view,
are all we've ever needed
to make our dreams come true.

Parents to look up to,
a home with comforts ease,
unwinding and relaxing
it's a place to shoot the breeze.
This paradise we take for granted
the flowers, rocks and trees,
oceans, seas, lakes and streams,
so full of energy.

Fresh air to fill our nostrils,
spring water here and there,
a treasure to hold on to
as I'm sure most are aware.
What a glorious life we all could lead
if ego was neutral based,
all souls running on positive ground
God's pride - the 'Human Race'.

Ambitions and Goals

We are strong and courageous
when we have self-esteem,
the flow of life's energy
is at times quite extreme.
Our hopes and our dreams
inspire ambitions and goals,
we strive for the best
our focus controlled.

Challenges are met
and obstacles overcome,
with belief in ourselves
the job can be done.
Helping others is a blessing
for more good comes our way,
the Universe is awesome
for we've a chance to repay.

Any kindness that's been given
the aide of a helping hand,
we've been the receiver
it's now time to expand.
Pass it on to others
bring a smile to someone's face,
bit by bit you'll realize
bad Karma's been erased.

Spread love with intention
encourage with ease,
give them back self-esteem
so they too can find peace.
The flow of life's energy
is at times quite extreme,
excitement tends to overflow
when we follow our dreams.

Angel

She'd meet us at the door each night,
then dance around in pure delight.

Excitement grew - it filled the air,
waiting until we'd take a chair.

One paw up - she was on her way,
coming home always made her day.

Soon she'd be curled up on your lap,
set to take a little nap.

No effort for contentment's gain,
a place in heart she does retain.

A Collie and Springer Spaniel mix,
her hair so soft and fine and thick.

She always seemed to walk with grace,
proud features upon her delicate face.

So many expressions from mouth, ears and eyes,
the look she would give as she'd let out a sigh.

She almost seemed human in action and thought,
and so many times she tried to talk.

We were lucky to have her; she was gentle and kind,
with so many friends who enjoyed spending time.

Now that she's gone from earth's fine restraints,
perhaps she brings comfort to the Angels and Saints.

Up in the 'Heavens' another 'Angel' sings true,
though still in the hearts of many in Sioux.

Atmosphere of Peace

Is it not better
to rise above Self,
to know your true Being
and personal wealth.
Entertain yourself freely
with visions and thought,
for answers are given
when they're honestly sought.

Most dreamers are fascinated
in a world of their own,
as the mind tends to lend them
a comfort zone.
Intentional meditation
in an atmosphere of peace,
enhances calm emotion
as stress is released.

It takes a few minutes
out of the day,
to relax all your muscles
and regain right-of-way.
Shaking off the negative
with lightness of soul,
as positive insights
inspire new goals.

Give thanks to your being
give thanks to your soul,
give thanks for a lifetime
of achievements and goals.
Whether at home, in the workplace,
the market, or en route,
a new bounce to your step
makes your voice want to shout.

Awesome Gift

A kindred spirit you touch a cord,
that would keep most anyone
from becoming bored.
A well lit flame who tends to uplift,
you're an Angel on earth
with an awesome gift.
You make people smile or laugh right out loud,
your humor seems to vanquish
any hint of a cloud.
Dark days are over when you come into sight,
folks know they are up
for one heck of a night.
Witty, smart and compassionate you do play the crowd,
and go about as far
as what is allowed.
You know what to say at any given time,
and comebacks are easy
you could spin on a dime.
Most people love you and admire your stance,
a wide range of topics
is not left to chance.
For you read to remember, you research for facts,
you don't let your wisdom
fall through the cracks.
You're a well lit flame who tends to uplift,
an Angel on earth
with an awesome gift.

Bingo

This is a game that requires no skill,
except to keep up with the Caller at will.

In the beginning the 'Early Birds' sell fairly fast,
the worker's sell many once the spell has been cast.

Once a Bingo's been called and the winnings doled out,
more and more 'Early Birds' are sold without doubt.

Most like to warm-up and play all they can,
before the crowd comes in and competition is scanned.

With too many people the odds of splitting go up,
but at least it still covers the coffee in their cup.

Two Squares or a Bowtie, Two Lines or a Kite,
the Wee House or Small Cross – that's dabbed in our flight.

The Empty House or Full House that's played for a win,
the Lucky Seven, the Arrow or Fifty-Fifty to fill in.

The Six Pack, the Nine Pack, the Top Corners and Line,
the letter V, X or T as the numbers combine.

The Odds and Evens are accumulated all through the night,
as well as the Five Star and Loonie Pot which tend to excite.

The G Ball's another that tends to build high,
that's when the Bingo Hall fills and intensifies.

Oh, to scream BINGO is a Bingo Players dream,
especially when the Pot's are so big and extreme.

Born with a Purpose

Born with a purpose all souls progress,
the flow of life's energy brings with it few tests.

For temptation may tease you or ego may reign,
then the good from all lessons goes right down the drain.

When pride leads you onwards with no thoughts of regret,
you may find that your soul has attracted much dept.

And remember if greed takes over your mind,
you can't take it with you it's not in our design.

If you've taken life for granted - quit while you're ahead,
back-track and re-focus on your purpose instead.

We're here for a reason - GOD gave us life,
it may be to raise a child or be a husband or wife.

A teacher, a writer or a hard-working man,
to learn and advance as fast as we can.

Forging ahead we grow cautious and wise,
following intuition all senses applied.

For each and every pathway there's a fork in the road,
with decisions to be made as we carry our load.

A good heart and clear conscience an understanding of ways,
a lifetime of wonder to enjoy day by day.

A thread of compassion as love leads the blind,
onward to Glory guided by the Divine.

Bugs

Bugs be gone you drive me nuts,
I'm forever slapping bruises,
sunburns and cuts.

You escape the full force of my frustration and wrath,
then soon find me again
further on down the path.

When both hands are busy in the dirt pulling weeds,
or while carrying rocks
you swarm in to feed.

My arms are the target as blood vessels bulge,
you tend to get greedy
and overindulge.

Then call in reinforcements once your bellies are full,
little devils with tactics
much like a pit-bull.

You leave my skin itchy with a lot of wee bumps,
which is better I guess
than a sting and a lump.

Mosquitoes, no-see-ums horseflies and wasps,
to be rid of you suckers would be
well worth the cost.

Unfortunately, I've never found anything that works,
I wonder if I'll notice once they
drive me berserk!

Bulges

When bodies take leave and lay loose for awhile,
gone are the clothes that fit with such style.
Opting for tee shirts, sweat shirts, and jeans,
or buying bigger sizes once you've stretched the inseam.
Joggers and shorts hold a lot of appeal,
especially when there's something you wish to conceal.
Dresses and loungers or loose comfy wraps,
help hide the bulges that end up on your lap.
Hidden from sight and put out of your mind,
until another few pounds sneak up from behind.

I guess the old saying, 'drink water and move',
is worth investigating – things are bound to improve.
Well balanced meals as portions provide,
be true to yourself and you'll soon trim your sides.
Each action that follows brings life up to speed,
for your body's now receiving just what it needs.
More energy will follow once things are in place,
and all fats and toxins are washed out and erased.
With a bit of 'will power' and 'positive thought',
you can use imagination to challenge soft spot's.

A sweet tooth, a craving, a snack that goes wild,
or comfort foods that calm your innermost child.
A new way of living and feeling alive,
the sense of accomplishment once you finally arrive.
Rewards surely follow as you'll require new clothes,
and of course boots and shoes for slimmed heels and toes.
New habits are formed as the old ones are dropped,
and in no time at all you'll be ready to shop.
The possibilities are endless; it's worth every cent,
once the mind and the body connect and consent.

Calm took Control

She sat on the hill, arms crossed on her knees,
watching the waves
that flowed gently with ease.
Patterns and shadows, reflections and glare,
all were acknowledged
as she continued to stare.
The sound of the water pampered her soul,
stress left her body
as calm took control.
The scent of Mother Nature unique in the wild,
allowed belief in her being
a Cosmic child.
Privileged and granted, sweet time on her own,
the earth was a playground
for all to call home.
When you take out the politics, disaster and strife,
hunger, pain and anguish
– it's a pretty good life.
She watched a young eagle soar through the sky,
unaware of the War
or the heartfelt cries.
The water continued its rhythmic beat,
as she slowly got up
and stood on her feet.
She looked to the sky and said a quick prayer,
for all those who suffered
in sorrow and despair.
Wishing them comfort in their time of need,
with the Spirit of Mother Nature
and a bit of God's speed.

Casper

Casper sits in a class all on its own,
while ghostly writings help set the tone.

Stylish, comfy, cozy, unique,
traveling with influence from the Captains seat.

Moving ever so gently while gracing the lake,
leaving behind us a smooth and even wake.

Sight-seeing in comfort and enjoying the view,
of land, water and nature so abundant around 'Sioux'.

The 'First Mate' is priceless, a treasure on board,
creating great meals from food stocked or stored.

Barbecuing the finest to perfection's own taste,
with food such as this – there isn't much waste.

She's one heck of a catch for both Captain and Craft,
her touch enhances ambiance as much as her laugh.

Boarding this vessel means you're in for a treat,
for Casper and Crew are sure to tickle your feet.

I mean you'll start talking and chuckling with ease,
whether fishing or eating – all stress seems to leave.

Upon docking, your land-legs may be tricky to find,
as you follow the pathway that the flowers define.

Left feet may follow you home when you leave,
for when trying to walk, you may otherwise weave.

All in all a great time is always enjoyed,
once the crew on the Casper shout 'Ahoy'.

Chain of Emotions

Dealt a hand to get through life
as obstacles fall into place,
I put up my chin and carry on
determination etched on my face.
I've had a glimpse of evil
at times I've feared for my life,
felt the sting of rejection
and pain like a two-sided knife.
I've felt both grief and sorrow
been opened to jealousy and spite,
been touched with love and betrayal
– many lessons within my sight.
I've walked on air and rode on clouds
as heartstrings played a tune,
soared to heights unknown to me
as if in a hot air balloon.
I've felt the pride of motherhood
and the joy of a fine career,
the blessing of great friendships
and peace as it often appears.
Creative thoughts residing
– the mind always on the go,
writing, crafting or placing rocks
– I push myself to grow.
Books are a major attraction
and they're keen to touch my hand,
instinct draws me to them
and I read 'til I understand.
Being of a sensitive nature
and having much love to give,
I send it out to nature
and the place where I now live.
A continuing chain of emotions
as life goes on it's ride,
each persons journey differs
from those standing by their side.

Cheap Thrills

(Glen)

Well, you've made it to thirty by the hair of your chin,
I'd say you were lucky
for your chances were slim.
Flying down backwards in a jeep on a hill,
- you boys will do anything
to get a cheap thrill.

The look on your faces were priceless I'll bet,
something neither one of you
will ever forget.
Then out on the snow machine – you and J.C.,
testing your handlebars
with the force of your knees.

I've heard of bending steal on a vice with some heat,
but on a frozen marker
– now that's rather unique.
You didn't need all that power on tracks or on wheels,
your spirited 'Inner Child'
ensures you don't heal.

It next took you down to the gym with the boys,
no thought to your age
or to the place you were employed.
Muscles and ligaments pulled out of place,
but nothing it seems
wipes the smile off your face.

Good natured and hardy – Newfoundlanders are tough,
or maybe they don't realize
when enough is enough.
We've enjoyed all your antics down at the Inn,
but Lord Lovin' Jesus
– your lucks running thin.

Child of the Universe

Child of the Universe so innocent and free,
truth still fresh within your mind; the things that you must see.
Closest to our Creator and His Angels in Heaven above,
sent to learn your lessons in compassion and in love.
Beliefs have not yet drawn the fog that puts you in the mist,
ideas, thoughts and all these things to you do still exist.
The joy, the play, the happiness; the link that brings us light,
vibrations that soon energize your spirits blissful right.
All things you learn from here on in may change your inner soul,
and strip away that part of you that makes our Beings whole.
For when you live without Intent, life just floats on by,
confusion becomes a part of you as other senses are denied.
Dimensions and realities held fast within your dream,
witness to your own beliefs – you'll raise your self-esteem.
By then all lessons taught through time – mans thoughts of right and wrong,
developed deep within your psyche; fear and doubt now tag along.
Inner wisdom – your guide to bliss is forgotten and rusty with age,
your Beings true potential is locked up in a shadowy cage.
Your Mind soon closes tightly as you turn from Spiritual belief,
your connection with the Universe gets undermined and then debriefed.
Ministers and Priest's who by the Book taught with control,
like Kings they ruled the people not fully grasping their Sacred role.
Gifted folk and those who knew were stoned and beaten with disgust,
drowned or burned upon a stake for there was much distrust.
If only they who taught the words that were written in His Book,
had taken time to realize the knowledge they mistook.
To go within and seek the Lord and know Him well and true,
just simple meditation and a different point of view.
Close your mind to scattered thoughts and seek the Lord within,
a journey that takes practice and of course self-discipline.
Have intent and focus on your 3rd eye's inner sight,
visions will soon come to pass along with Love and Light.
Child of the Universe so innocent and free,
perhaps in time our schools will teach our true identity.
Then peace on Earth will flourish – once folks join to conform,
He's by our side both night and day to weather any storm.

Chores

A women's work is never done,
for they clean up after everyone.

They do the dishes, vacuum, and dust,
then scrub the bathrooms inner crust.

Make the beds and then strip them down,
tackle the laundry all around.

Water plants and fix the snacks,
without a thank you or pat on the back.

Arrange all the schedules; cook, clear and bake,
there to compliment and congratulate.

Shop for groceries; carry them out and then in,
disperse of all items before supper begins.

Help out with most problems, sew and repair,
work in tight circles as chores repeat here and there.

Most have careers on top of this load,
as they multi-task through life deciphering codes.

Immeasurable wisdom absorbed and maintained,
along with new energy that runs through their veins.

Driven to challenge - to prove and perfect,
their labor, their love, and their intellect.

Most even manage to retain humor's wit,
once the chores are all done and they've a moment to sit.

Chosen Path

I feel there is something that I have yet to do,
I sense that I am guided
but all the same still feel confused.
I follow my chosen path through life – a journey much progressed,
with a love for reading and writing
thoughts and feelings have no rest.
For there are lessons I must learn and people I must meet,
so many obstacles to overcome
with fears that have cold feet.
I know I need to go within and connect with my inner self,
relax and let my world unwind
as ego sits on the shelf.
So far I've been very lucky, at times I've even felt blessed,
with the folks put on my path through life
who've inspired and who've impressed.
I've learned a lot of lessons – a few were absorbed rather fast,
the experience and knowledge
feeds both my present and my past.
I understand much of what happens due to the mind's analyzing ways,
I know what most folks are thinking
for with each action – emotion's displayed.
This comes in a range of signals; body language, their stance and their eyes,
you see it in those you meet everyday
and in those who just pass by.
In tune with my body's awareness – alert in the daytime and night,
intuition and inner gut feelings
help shed a lot of insight.
Dreams also lead to answers even though I've no questions to ask,
like a slap in the face, they keep me awake
in wonder of the human mask.
They say all things will come to light when following destiny's trail,
each step you take helps to navigate
your future and what it entails.

Clan Society

Each Clan had a Chief, who lived like a King,
ruling over his properties and the goods it would bring.
When a Chiefs son came to manhood he was carefully observed,
the Clans loyalty and respect were held in reserve.
Quick to revenge and able to lead,
he was accepted as worthy enough to succeed.
But if living on the Continent had softened his mind,
and his sedentary interests were all they could find.
He would be much despised and their allegiance would turn,
to a younger brother with the strength and the skill to discern.
The loyalties of the Clan once given were strong,
ancient stories of Valor were soon put to song.
Only half of the Clanship had profitable work,
though all were expected to carry Broadsword and Dirk.
All males were Soldiers from the young to the old,
rank was fixed by Social Status and easily controlled.
The Chief was the Coronal; he held the Clans fear,
sons and brothers commanded the flanks and the rear.
The Sergeant or Officers were from the heads of each home,
sons, brothers and tenants formed Platoons of their own.
All families stood in Battle in much the same way,
according to Clan importance, all placements were made.
Brother fought beside brother and father by son,
witnessing valor and courage once the war had begun.
The Chief wasn't distinguished by his fortune or dress,
but by the cattle on his Braes and men on request.
With the Chief rode his henchmen, his brothers and guard,
and for recording their history – the hereditary Bard.
He sat on a hillside observing the Battle and Chief,
an epic poem in the making of both bravery and grief.
The McCrimmons thus followed with bagpipes and flute,
to lift the fighting spirits of the Clansmen on route.
The Bladier was the Adviser and Lawyer on hand,
the Spokesman on all issues including Strategic War plans.
The men and chiefs servants carried swords, axes and bows,
some preferred muskets so had their powder in tow.
With Juniper in their Badges and 'Hold Fast' in their cries,
Clan tartans gave them strength and a strong sense of Pride.

Confederation College

Confederation College gave my fears a place to roam,
away from friends and family and the place that I call home.

Moving from town to city – double-lanes and traffic lights,
pedestrians and bicycles always in peripheral sight.

The College was overwhelming it seemed I was always lost,
many times the hallways were checked and then were double-crossed.

I met some wonderful people – the Professors were all great,
and the class-mates that I hung with are friends I appreciate!

We covered much material and ventured both near and far,
mostly to fine restaurants and a few times to the Bar.

Mario's and Montana's, Mr. Chinese and the Reserve,
the food was overwhelming adding nicely to our curves.

Each day brought new adventures – forgotten formulas or skills,
but somehow we got through it thanks to the younger girls goodwill.

They flew through all their lessons understanding the lingo and keys,
I admired all their knowledge about the computers vast mysteries.

Yes, Confederation College gave my fears a place to roam,
until I finally lost them all before returning home.

Connected to This Power

*He of good fortune
has God on his side,
for when connected to this power
you have peace inside.
For He's the almighty
our hope and our strength,
He's brought about miracles
and left us with Saints.
He's allowed us Free Will
for both want and desire,
sacrificed His own Son
for all sins to expire.
His love and compassion
flows to each soul,
our lifeblood and conscience
are part of this whole.
Made in his likeness
our spirits burn bright,
meditation allows us
an inner soul flight.
To connect with this power
for visions own sake,
as it strengthens our belief's
and lessens heartache.
Yes, he of good fortune
has God on his side,
a sense of well-being
and a feeling of Pride.*

Consequence

Consequence has a way
of stepping on toes,
for what goes around, comes around
as everyone knows.
It may take a while
or no time at all,
for the past and the present
to become closely involved.
So watch P's and Q's
bite your tongue – walk away,
for thoughts, words and actions
will haunt future days.
The most important lesson
that life has to teach,
is Love and Compassion
for the souls we meet.
Respecting all people,
their possessions, their homes,
not only for their sake
but also our own.
Don't destroy, steal or sabotage,
hurt, maim or curse,
for what's put out in the atmosphere
returns a bit worse.
I've seen some broken-hearted,
heard of cabins burning down,
bad luck surrounding couples
as bad Karma comes to town.
If you think no-one is watching
and you've gotten off scot-free,
think again for the Universe
is connected to you and me.
Yes, consequence has a way
of stepping on toes,
so think before your actions
and justice come nose to nose.

Coronation Street

I've watched Coronation Street year after year,
and enjoyed all the episodes
as they have appeared.
From Monday to Friday all work stops at five,
I curl up on the sofa
as the show comes alive.
On Sundays I watch two and a half hours of bliss,
I work it round events
'cause it's a show I won't miss.
So when CBC intervenes for Olympics and Sports,
I ban the television
as a last resort.
I know this is petty but there's naught I can do,
I should have taped every episode
so I could review.
Like an addict I need my fix everyday,
and on weekends it's party time
– I love the role play.
Hindsight is wonderful – could you imagine my wealth,
if I had every episode
up on a shelf.
For this is a series I could watch all day long,
the cast is fantastic
– realistic and strong.
Characters blending in everyday scenes,
perfect for the parts
they play on the screen.
Thanks to the Producers and all others involved,
for the way it's been written
and all mysteries solved.
It holds me spellbound – I don't answer the phone,
for when Coronation Street airs
I prefer being alone.

Depression Comes Home

Drained and abandoned
a life lived alone,
from daylight to darkness
depression comes home.
You see other couples
holding hands on the street,
or racing home to their loved ones
whom they can't wait to greet.
Expressions of passion
a taunt or a tease,
knowing their goals
are to cherish and please.
Ignoring their pleasure
is a short term relief,
for you can shut it all out
as you bottle your grief.
But it's there in the office
or out on the floor,
and again on the TV
once you've secured all your doors.
A GOD given instinct
to love and be loved,
so pick yourself up
and give your soul a shove.
Shake some sense into being
and give depression the boot,
slap a smile on your face
someone might think you're cute.
Put yourself out there
give romance a chance,
lighten your heart
and let your sweet soul dance.

Double-Dip

Blessed with visions on Moose Lake Road,
I was one of many truckers hauling load after load.
After months of construction I'd yet to see a moose,
I asked the Lord to show me one amongst the pine and spruce.
I didn't have to go too far when one came into sight,
around an 'S'-shaped corner in the ditch off to the right.
A beautiful majestic bull, its hide - a dark chocolate brown,
the sunlight caught his antlers just before he turned round.
Taking off through wild alders, I just couldn't believe my eyes,
no trace of him existed nor destruction for his size.
Next was an Albino moose rumored 'big and white',
I asked the Lord just one more time to bring it into sight.
Blessed with another vision not a mile down the road,
I slowed the 'Mack' to a standstill as excitement overflowed.
Across the barren field near the bush on the other side,
was the bull making his departure looking so dignified.
I pulled the air horn gently which made a moaning sound,
and was out of the truck in no time as he slowly turned around.
I stood on the edge of the roadway right behind the truck,
as he cautiously walked towards me - I couldn't believe my luck.
Not ten feet from my presence he let me observe his stance,
an Albino moose with a silver nose and pink eyes that seemed to dance.
I stood in awe of all I saw my attention level was high,
I felt a surge of energy that came from his power supply.
We observed each other for quite awhile before he turned to leave,
a sense of respect and honor seemed to wash right over me.
I've heard that when aligned with one no matter how it occurs,
a unique and sacred energy soon begins to stir.
To some they are Sacred Beings, God-like in a sense,
it's taboo to harm these Albinos for all they represent.
That about explains all the emotions I felt upon that day,
I know that God was with me as He answered right away.
I'm forever counting blessings that catch me in their grip,
especially when out in nature - as I tend to double-dip.

Double Rainbow

While on our way to Thunder Bay
my sister and I witnessed a sight,
– a beautiful double rainbow
with one end on the hoods upper right.
We focused in on each other
excitement shone through our eyes,
then back to the lakes calm center
where the rainbow appeared to divide.

One pointed straight towards the city
the other – on the hood of the car,
miles seemed to pass in disbelief
as it guided like a shining star.
I'm sure our 'Mother' was with us
for she knew we were on our way,
and being in and out of body
it seemed possible she'd meet us that day.

For when pain overtakes the body
– the soul can often depart,
leaving the patient in fevered state
with a slower beating of the heart.
The ancients believed that rainbows
were a bridge between Heaven and Earth,
a symbol of divine communication
a good sign for all it is worth.

For others the myth of 'a Pot of Gold'
at the end of the rainbows trail,
still holds true and strong today
though its seekers have always failed.
I've never heard of a single soul
coming close to this mystical pot,
but there it was not two feet away
on the hood giving food for thought.

Dream Venture

One night while I was dreaming – my visions seemed so real,
my girl friend Cora and myself were playing in a field.
Instead of who we are right now – two boys came into view,
living in a time long past – our clothes were far from new.
Caps, knickers and suspenders – high socks and ankle boots,
old and worn, but rather comfy as we followed the old horse route.
It took us to the Marina which was then a Trader's shack,
and I bartered with a man over the potatoes that were safe within my sack.
Next thing I knew we were elevating – up towards the sky,
without the flapping of our arms or fear within our eyes.
I noticed a great big hole in the toe of Cora's boot,
but this surprised me not at all for we were both destitute.
On through the ozone – our bodies seemed to float,
I looked back down upon the earth and took some mental notes.
Then slowly we descended – down from this Heavenly state,
I had to protect both eyes and ears with no time for debate.
The POP, POP I heard within my head proved all instincts were right,
I chuckled to myself at that and this odd dream throughout the night.
We landed by the Marina as gentle as could be,
then kicked a ball down Wellington – our spirits were rather free.
We made our way to the High School and entered through the door,
scanned the rooms and hallways as we walked across the floor.
We passed some basketball players as they dribbled in the gym,
and then met up with Sharon doing aerobics to keep herself slim.
Next, a man playing a 'Viol' in hat and suit and tie,
handed me his keychain filled with stones that caught my eye.
As we went outside the doors at last – our genders had been replaced,
a few years older or so it seemed and with a touch of grace.
Wearing old-fashioned dresses with bonnets over curls– we were very much at ease,
we said good-bye and she took her leave as I sat down for some tea.
The cup was huge and I poured from a gourd with no handle or lid on top,
as it spilt – I took a look around and saw a woman coming with a mop.
Then an Asian girl stood in my view, her father – a few feet back,
with his cowboy boot up on the fence – I felt a slight panic attack.
The stagecoach arrived with dust in the air as the girl begged me to stay,
I turned and smiled as best I could then I boarded without delay.
Alas, before the pyramids – I bargained for Alien stones,
as a giant dictionary was covered with scribbles and color tones.
I couldn't believe they didn't leave more of the treasures they were lucky to find,
but of course I took what was offered – 'cause the rocks were one of a kind.
The mind – it has no limits once imagination takes its flight,
a time for great adventures as you dream throughout the night.

Dunvegan Castle

The Seat of the MacLeod Chiefs for centuries gone by,
is Dunvegan Castle on the Isle of Skye.
A massive stronghold still situated on a spur of hard rock,
rising thirty feet high from the shores of the Loch.
Surrounded on three sides by water and on four sides by ghosts,
MacLeod portraits leave a lineage of possible hosts.
Along with relics and furniture, a lock of Prince Charlie's hair,
is the 7th Century 'Fairy Flag' which is most delicate and rare.
The Castle's endured many battles and fought the elements of time,
thirty Chiefs in succession of a direct family line.
Majestic and powerful this fortress stands, invulnerable to Clan attack,
obtained in the 13th Century by the son of Olaf the Black.
'Leod' and his Lady had two sons of their own,
'Tormod' and 'Torquil' played in this Castle of stone.
Chiefs down through the ages have remodeled to taste,
adding rocks to the structure architecturally placed.
Battlement blocks had been joined in long angular form,
the 'Great Keep' was used as Dungeon Tower and Dorm.
Private apartments, bed chambers as well as the 'Great Hall',
in the fifty foot Tower with ten foot thick walls.
The 1500's brought the 'Fairy Tower'; it was built by design,
the idea and the work of the 8th Chief in line.
The impressive Piper's Gallery honors this man,
as Founder of the College for Macleod's Bag-Piping Clan.
That would be the McCrimmons' who've composed and piped all these years,
putting to music all the Clan's hopes, dreams and tears.
Our heritage, our history, our Ancestral pride,
took root at Dunvegan on the Isle of Skye.

Echo

An echo through time
as memory unwinds,
though dim and faded
eyes sparkle and shine.

With the joy of the moment
or regrets solemn tear,
the "what ifs" and "maybes"
do often appear.

Paths tend to wander
and lives tend to change,
journey's through life
may get re-arranged.

Fate intervenes
every now and again,
delivering someone or something
to keep us entertained.

Time travels onwards
as we take a look back,
and all captured memories
are there for feedback.

Unique in our structure
our minds come alive,
privy to information
in our living archive.

An Echo through time
as memory unwinds,
though dim and faded
eyes sparkle and shine.

Ellen

You shine your light so brightly
on the world and all it's cares,
Mother Nature's met her match
for you alleviate despair.

Eagerly helping your fellow man
their families and their pets,
helping to raise the funds they need
to provide a safety net.

Though known as a Comedienne
by millions coast to coast,
you stand alone on a pedestal
much loved as a TV Host.

All guests are quite amazing
as is the talent on each show,
you motivate the audience
with that special Cover Girl glow.

Down to earth and natural
very unique in your stance,
for who else on this planet
could inspire the world to Dance.

A child of the Universe
spreading love like a breath of fresh air,
you're one of God's great messengers
for the world needs intensive care.

To live, to love, to laugh and dance
to inspire, learn and grow,
five days a week you entertain
as your gentle nature flows.

Entrapment

Take a normal person, who's of a rational mind,
introduce them to a stranger
who treats them well and kind.
Drawn to the compelling mask that's worn and on display,
both charming and adoring
they'll find they're swept away.
Caught up in the whirlwind often referred to as love,
until the mask begins to slip
and a push becomes a shove.
Temper tantrums flaring – true nature comes to light,
conversation follows
as to instigate a fight.
It usually starts with little things until jealousy climbs on board,
the mind games then take over
as Ego tends to soar.
Negativity follows suit as happiness tends to fade,
common sense doesn't stand a chance
as nerves are raw and frayed.
Love will hold them captive and fear will tear them apart,
all hopes of living a normal life
will be as shattered as their hearts.
At last a tiny shell appears beaten and forlorn,
this normal person stands alone
as other folk may scorn.
So walk in the shoes of the beaten, carry a torch with no flame,
feel the shattered nerves inside
and hope you don't go insane.
For no-one could possibly imagine the loss of power and loss of will,
at times the only light they see
is from their windowsill.
Jesus comes to those who call from deep within their minds,
His Love and His protection
are soon there for them to find.
Comforting with an unseen quilt that wraps them tight and warm,
peace of mind soon comes to rest
as they weather out the storm.

Entwined

Earthly Spirits pass us by,
as knowledge becomes
more magnified.

Nature surrounds us nurturing our souls,
spirit guides us onward
to much higher goals.

When concept and understanding open new books,
thoughts and intuitions
are given second looks.

When closed doors are opened they too will then see,
unwritten but experienced
by simple folk like me.

I've had premonitions and dreams that came true,
experiences with butterflies
and flowers that bloomed.

I've been led to some rocks with messages from above,
for our Lord and my parents
I have a great love.

I'm very open minded needing neither proof nor print,
I talk from my experience
of separate incidents.

Believe or disbelieve me it really matters naught,
for I have all the evidence
with each and every rock.

So keep your senses open to the Universal Mind,
both worlds are connected
to all that is Divine.

I leave no room for sceptics perhaps speaking out of line,
but all experiences - I believe
because of course they're mine.

Escape

There are good days and bad days
happy ones and sad,
carefree or anxious
there are many moods to be had.
But it doesn't seem to matter
whatever my state,
getting back into nature
always feels so great.
The visions of beauty
calm both body and soul,
with the scent in the air
when out for a stroll.
The shimmering water
is the ultimate attraction,
letting go of cares and worries
to the minds satisfaction.
Inspiration wakes up
– senses keen and alive,
I feel empowered
with a new inner drive.
I've had many visitors
so natural and wild,
approach while I'm working
perhaps judging my style.
Whatever the reason
I've enjoyed every one,
except for the snakes
`they put me on the run'.
The squirrels and ravens
I love to observe,
on the whole – this life style
is good for the nerves.

Face to the Wind

I've washed away
all of yesterdays doubts,
along with the fears
that I'd knocked about.

Not a care in the world
no sense of regret,
I nurtured free spirit
right out of neglect.

Onward I've traveled
face to the wind,
gained my high school diploma
through self-discipline.

Confederation College
and a home away from home,
met a lot of great people
as I stood on my own.

Even drove in the city
without getting lost,
except for one adventure
as the roads had been crossed.

And sometimes the Universe
has stepped in to define,
personal goals
that I've left far behind.

Onward and upward
my spirit takes flight,
another new challenge
with interests unite.

No time for boredom
no time to rest,
as I reach for the stars
and give them my best.

Family Ties

Intrigued with lives lived in the past,
my family tree
is growing fast.
I learn a little and at times a lot,
required is patience
more often than not.
To know each persons name and place,
of the ancestor's that
I'd like to trace.
Where they worked and what they did,
hobbies they had
and the lives that they lived.
In England the Corbett's and Weaver's did run,
a line of descendants
right down to my mom.
'Morton Corbet, a place where the goats now roam wild,
is a castle in ruins for which
many claims have been filed.
Her mother married John Oliver Payne,
then immigrated to Canada
and here they remained.
'The Isle of Skye' a Scottish domain,
is where some of my
fathers family remain.
Dunvegan Castle is the seat of the MacLeod's,
of which I might add
I am very proud.
So I write lots of letters receiving pictures and tales,
picking up on and tracing
my ancestors trails.
One day I will travel and with people I'll talk,
and hopefully I'll pass
where my ancestors walked.
I know it sounds crazy – an impossible feat,
but it's an interesting hobby
for each person's unique.

Famous Artists

There are many famous Artists with styles that set them apart,
in the late eighteen hundreds Impressionism first got its start.
In the 70's and 80's it had hit its peak,
these early Artists had a talent that was different and unique.
There was Claude Monet and Augusta Renoir,
and Henri De Toulouse known for paintings of Bars.
Along with the night scenes, catching moments as they came,
the Circus too inspired him for he made himself quite a name.
Edgar Degas and Eduard Manet, Mark Cassatt and Paul Cézanne,
were very serious about their paintings as are their many fans.
Visual Art became part of life – capturing moments in time and space,
these Artists left a part of themselves to cherish and to embrace.
Post Impressionism was also inspiring for many Artists of that time,
a few of them are Famous now though they died within their prime.
Vincent Van Gough was born in '48 and died in 1903,
his subject matter was ordinary life and his Paintings are something to see.
Another one was Paul Gauguin, who lived a tragic life,
depressed, alone and unlucky in love for when he died – he had no wife.
He was a Dealer, Merchant, and Philosopher – rebellious in his own way,
he was also a hopeless Romantic who 'took his life with a gun' one day.
In the early 1900's, Fauvism took the world by storm,
brightness seemed to rule supreme and primary colors were the norm.
Henri Matisse lived from '69 until 1954,
he believed in the simplification of forms; the 'essentials' and no more.
Patterns and the flatness of shapes was a new form of Art back then,
color expressed emotion and mood with a rush of adrenalin.
Psychological implications lent its name to the Paintings in view,
'Fauves' means 'The Wild Beasts' and perhaps got misconstrued.
André Derain lived until 1954 and was originally taught by Cézanne,
but soon he followed Matisse's Style and 'Fauvism' soon began.

Fanti-Physio

May, June, and July of two thousand and five,
Thunder Bay was the destiny to which I did arrive.
The Valhalla Inn was my residence, my home,
while attending Physio all on my own.

Each day a taxi arrived by the door,
to escort me to sessions on the bench or the floor.
Kangus Sauna was the building, Fanti-Physio the place,
where stretch, exercise and acupuncture were tried 'just in case'.

Rob was amazing; he works from the mind,
imagination changed everything, it helped me unwind.
I focused on the muscles that were giving me grief,
but unfortunately it was only a short term relief.

With that and the exercise, the belt and the ball,
I was hoping all pain would quickly dissolve.
His associates were assigned other clients on hand,
bikes, balls, and weights were arranged with a plan.

They kept pretty busy and got along great,
I'd highly recommend them to rehabilitate.
The receptionists were friendly - both down to earth,
easy to talk to and full of wisdom and mirth.

Both Sharon and Michelle became more like friends,
I looked forward to our visits right up to the end.
I left each a rose bush to plant in their yards,
and for Rob, a bamboo plant, a squirrel and card.

I'd also crocheted a doily more like a throw,
with two cherubs representing his children in tow.
From stranger, to friendships, to a part of the past,
memories are precious and I know they will last.

Fate

Could life be a test
or a trial
or such,
people advancing
or failing
at touch.
Whatever we do
a judge
there awaits,
deciding upon
our destiny
- our fate.
Getting put down
at some
of life's turns,
there are millions
of things
being taught
just to learn.
Self-satisfaction
and a feeling
of pride,
are all
that we need
and they're found
deep inside.
So hold onto your dreams,
ambitions
and goals
be true
to yourself
and your life
will be whole.

Fears

People are people no matter their race,
each have a weak spot at times hard to face.
Insecurities too numerous to even begin,
shape each individual from somewhere within.
Through the years they nurture the fears that they know,
hidden and protected they continue to grow.

Until one day they're crippled overcome it appears,
unwilling to challenge the source of their fears.
Some become prisoners in their own homes,
terrified of people and the unknown.
With others its heights or feeling boxed in,
anxiety builds as the panic begins.

For some it is snakes, spiders and mice,
or even something simple like water or ice.
People are people no matter their race,
at some point in time they'll have fears to face.
It goes without saying instincts help us survive,
and fear is a part of what keeps us alive.

But at times it inhibits personal growth and appeal,
and if left unattended life becomes an ordeal.
Stress is a factor that touches all souls,
and it seems more abundant as you reach for your goals.
Learn to breath and relax then focus with intent,
find a place deep inside where you feel content.

People are people and we've all fears to face,
overcoming the obstacles can be hard to embrace.
But life's meant for living, to feel and observe,
to stand ready and waiting for the next curve.
With each goal you set, a new one arrives,
isn't it great to be well and alive?

First Love

Feelings
like the waters deep,
emotions
then upon you creep.

Pulling you
- the rapids soar,
another victim
to its score.

The under current
pulls at you still,
fighting against
all power of will.

Waves of love
tear you apart,
you know he's forever
in your heart.

Remembering
a crooked smile,
or eyes that
loved you for awhile.

Arms that gave
such tenderness,
a comfort
that you're going to miss.

Feelings
like the waters deep,
memories
that are yours to
keep.

Fishing

There's no such thing as a lonely fisherman
with the sky and the lake so blue,
rarely does he go alone,
for there's usually a buddy or two.
And if by chance the day is clear
and no-one is in sight,
the beauty and serenity
calms a Soul if wound too tight.
The pleasures in the fishing
– being out in a peaceful way,
reeling them in one by one
'til the limit calls it a day.
Home is where the heart is
especially if she's holding the pan,
ready for the beans and taters
and fresh fish by where she stands.
The taste is quite delicious
especially when hunger makes faint,
good at any temperature
a meal that would tempt a Saint.
Excellent hot with a meal
and cold when snacking takes place,
especially good in the winter time
just for a change of pace.
Frozen packs are quickly thawed
lightly floured and put to the pan,
fries and a can of Pork 'n' Beans
makes for a tasty meal plan.

Flickering Flames

Like flickering flames of a raging fire,
love tickles and teases
and lights sweet desire.

Walking on air – your whole body sings,
the right partner in life
can mean everything.

The sound of a voice; the laughter, the jokes,
a look or a smile
– a touch or a poke.

All senses alive as energy flows,
right through your body
and down to your toes.

For love is the answer to all of life's grief,
a giving of hearts
and new found beliefs.

For love conquers all and it's often been said,
this emotion, this feeling
brings peace where it's spread.

Can you imagine our world ruled with brotherly love,
–all nations would flourish
instead of needing to shove.

Life would be grand – no hunger or hate,
no wars or depletion
or crimes of the State.

Like flickering flames of a raging fire,
all hearts would unite
and all souls would inspire.

Free Reign

For centuries abusers have run with free reign,
intimidating others using force or disdain.
The mask of a charmer; deceptive and wise,
attracts souls to befriend or to victimize.
Some kind of 'radar' leads them into your space,
complimenting or praising a certain look on your face.
Gaining trust and compassion your sympathy is theirs,
soon the flaw in their make-up leaves you shattered and scared.
Much like setting a hook 'they reel you in',
confined and controlled
your new life begins.
Nightmares take over from the dreams in your past,
self-esteem is diminished the more you're harassed.
You become a mere shadow beaten and weak,
unable to think and unable to speak.
Fear and anxiety mixed with anger and rage,
builds over time as you pass through each stage.
Intensity renders you empty and numb,
for by now you're positioned well under the thumb.
Pride knows great shame once courage deserts,
though senses are sharpened
and put on alert.
There's no thought to the victims' ambitions or goals,
just a sweet sense of power and total control.
If this sounds familiar – run as fast as you can,
because this kind of love is just a 'flash in the pan'.
Once the Honeymoon's over true self interferes,
and as the charmer fades out a stranger appears.
Let intuition guide you to a well deserved path,
where love makes you want to sit up and laugh.
Life's meant for living though 'will' leads the way,
so watch, learn, and listen, don't be easy prey.
Take time to discover what's hidden from view,
because you're pretty special
and there's only one YOU!

Gestures & Sketches

Gestures are fast motion
a means of capturing time,
quick sketches of a movement
that is drawn on a dime.

Just a figure of speech of course
because you use a wee book,
it's like a memory picture
that you draw while taking a look.

It's a preliminary sketch
of a thumbnail print,
eyes, hand and pencil
quickly learn how to sprint.

Sketches are much different
for you're capturing a scene,
the structure is more solid
and finished in-between.

More time and care is given
with focus on detail,
intent – your hand keeps drawing
as you set the size to scale.

This takes time and effort
though some do have the skill,
to complete a perfect picture
that captures reality's view.

Gift of Friendship

The gift of friendship is one of life's pleasures,
to be honoured an valued
and very much treasured.

The friends that I have are one of a kind,
they are open and honest
– not easy to find.

The humour and laughter; the logic and wit,
is there with them always
– it just doesn't quit.

Each one is different though they blend naturally,
different jobs, different lives
and spirits that are free.

There's nothing like a gathering to help start the day,
conversation all around
with coffee on its way.

I know that I am lucky with friends such as these,
all time spent together
passes with ease.

Goldlund Mine '84

I was hired out at Goldlund in the spring of eighty-four,
my job was to load the grizzly with the freshly blasted ore.

I also did some clean up – swept the walkway to the cone,
and underneath the belts of course where fell the dust and stones.

I ran the little Case below in the yard outside the mill,
cleaning up discarded piles that the wheel barrels filled.

And when the trucks arrived on site to pick up the processed ore,
I'd load the bags with a special fork onto the flatbeds' floor.

Then one day my boss came to get me - he drove me down the road,
there was a huge cave opening where the trucks hauled load after load.

The stockpile was tremendous there wasn't much room left to dump,
beside it – an old bulldozer sat which had the mechanics stumped.

A mine with over 200 men and no one could angle the blade,
the mechanics and foreman left so I could take some time to play.

It took me about 20 minutes trying everything that came to mind,
it was older than I'd first imagined, in fact I'm sure 'one of a kind'.

By the time they returned to pick me up I had leveled all the piles,
all of them were grinning showing relief within their smiles.

That's probably what saved me from being cut when layoffs began,
for I was the only female who worked in the mill on hand.

Adele was their surveyor – she worked out in the field,
and Donna ran the office where I'm sure her humor appealed.

I enjoyed my time at Goldlund – it was a year I'll never forget,
the work was very interesting and so were the people I met.

Good Intentions

Our beginnings were spent with our parents
and our siblings before we left home,
for marriage, a career or to study and learn
for the world was theirs to roam.
Each day was a new adventure
or a drama for emotional souls,
we had interests and dreams and a lot of good friends
with ambitions to reach many goals.
Life sped up along the way
and time was limited by choice,
our friends came first to mingle and dance
and our parents had the quiet voice.
"Come visit more often" they'd smile and wave
we'd agree as we left them behind,
good intentions at times are swept away
for the young are often quite blind.
Looking back I realize it was the company they craved
for the family had become very small,
I wish I could cash all my good intentions in
for what they asked for cost nothing at all.
I feel the same as they did then
for my family has also dispersed,
at times I'm sad and lonely
but life pulls me in feet first.
As I have so many interests
my mind doesn't get much of a break,
from the depths of despair to off elsewhere
all woes are given a shake.
Luckily in my adult years
good sense seemed to buckle me down,
my parents became my mentors and friends
whom I loved to be around.
Still I regret some choices from the past
for both parents have now moved on,
together again side by side
with the Lord from daylight 'til dawn.
So prioritize your choices
and save yourself from regrets,
good intentions only take you so far
before finding you're deeply in dept.

Gossip

Gossip is
idleness at work,
causing disruption
anger and hurt.
Unhappy people
spreading the word,
each story gets bigger
the more it is heard.
For no matter how little
a person might know,
the demon inside them
helps the story to grow.
Few facts remain
in the tales they weave,
the more convincing they sound
many more will believe.
This is the balance
between friendship and foe,
on how far these stories
will actually go.
Vindictive people
through jealousy or spite,
sit on their pedestals
while thinking they're right.
Until one day it's their turn
to entertain the town,
the rumours and gossip
will soon bring them down.
There's a lesson to learn
as we travel through life,
to be happy and content
you must try to be nice.
For 'what you put out'
will one day return,
it's Karma's way of saying,
"You reap what you earn".

Great Gifts

The world
is so beautiful
– you need only
take a look,
the wildlife
that surrounds us
is like from
a story book.
The trees – so green
the sky, so blue
the stars
shining over head,
the water at times
like a mirror
and the grass
– a soft summer bed.
The mountains we climb
the hills we walk,
the rainbows
after a storm,
the moon that guides us
through the night
and the clouds
where pictures are formed.
All these things
and so much more
were given to us
with love,
so take a look
around yourself
these are gifts
from the good God above.

Griffith Mine

In nineteen hundred and eighty-five
during a contract with the CNR,
I hauled ore from the Griffith Mine stockpile
to the CN tracks to load empty cars.
The destination was the Red Lake crossing
a stockpile was made on sight,
to load the empties with cautious measure
for this product collected moisture at night.
A rainstorm would be a challenge
as the weight was hard to control,
a lot of figuring went into each bucket
on the articulating old loaders main hold.
Magnetite is the mineral form
of iron oxide and it's black as coal,
an important ingredient used in the process
of separating liquids in a dark circular hole.
It's weight provides division
for it settles in blanket-like state,
taking floaters to the bottom
and holding them down like an iron grate.
It's a really different substance
for if wet 'polarization' takes place,
when walking or trying to scoop it up
it quickly spreads out the opposite way.
When dry little clouds surround each step
a powdery dust tends to fill the air,
settling in and all over the equipment
as parts soon showed signs of wear.
It got right under your skin it seemed
no matter how hard you'd rub and scrub,
eventually it would work its way out
from feet right up to your mug.
I met a lot of really nice folks
as I traveled back and forth down the road,
gained experience on an eighteen wheeler
with the backing and dumping of numerous loads.

Half of a Whole

A Soul-mate
is one half of a whole,
there for you always
as your reach higher goals.
A person who connects,
understanding your needs,
and like nectar – their love
is what nurtures and feeds.
Taking pride in and respecting
loved ones with care,
a helping hand when it's needed
to fix or repair.

To share in the workload
– a companion for life,
whether or not
they're your husband or wife.

Someone to share meals,
the time and the cost,
if not then the balance
is ultimately lost.
Like anything in life
maintaining is the key,
otherwise it's a ride
one may be taking for free.
A Soul-mate is
one half of a whole,
you feel it in your Being
'cause your Heart's in the know.

His Fathers Eyes

Through the eyes of His Father – He understood man,
believing in love
and the law of the land.
Dedicated His life so that we could live ours,
I speak to Him often
as I look to the stars.
His heart was so pure, innocent and wise,
who better to see
through His Father's eyes.
He healed the crippled, the blind and diseased,
while carrying burdens
with grace and with ease.
Walking for miles in the heat of the day,
spreading the Gospel
and teaching to pray.
Exorcised demons from the bodies of man,
and offered God's Light
and His own helping hand.
He walked on the waters and calmed the storm,
so many miracles
this one Man performed.
Can you imagine if He was given free reign,
and not treated with jealousy
fear or distain.
I respect Him and love Him with honor and pride,
for the peace He has given me
deep down inside.
How proud His Father and Mother must be,
for things done in His name
throughout history.
And although I love life and the people I've known,
I can't wait to see Him
once I return home.

Horseback Riding

The first time I ever went for a ride upon a horses back,
was in Atikokan at the CNR before moving them down the track.
The men let them out for exercise and put us on for a ride,
my sister or friend went with me – as I was only four or five.
Next time was later in Sioux Lookout, while living on Government Row,
a friend and I went to Cedar Bay and for ten bucks we got to go.
Afterwards I was rather sore on the inside of ankles and knees,
not being a horseback rider I wore runners and an old pair of jeans.
Those couple of rides went rather well – no signs of danger or fear,
but that all changed in Winnipeg with my cousins in my seventeenth year.
I was to ride a tired old nag on a patch of Manitoba's' fine soil,
but before feet were in the stirrups, she was off like a wound up coil.
The guide seemed to take forever before coming into my sight,
I desperately hung onto the reins and mane because the horse was bent on flight.
This time I ached all over the place my muscles were tight from the fear,
that and the bones that had suffered, when came the meeting between saddle and rear.
It wasn't until many years later that I attempted this feat once again,
with Cheryl, Lynda, Lori and Justine – we road the vast terrain.
Then came a 'T' in the road up ahead, a left turn was what we sought.
when coming to the crossroads, all others had started to trot.
But my horse took off in full gallop, then suddenly turned to the bush,
myself – I was looking forward, so I wouldn't end up on my tush.
Then the saddle turned round his belly – I was now hanging upside down,
my feet were in the stirrups as a boulder shared my frown.
Not two feet from my opened eyes this nightmare finally stopped
thank goodness for the bush line, or my face would have met that rock.
We then travelled roads and alleys, had soup at Clarkes Cafe',
then once again we mounted up and Cheryl led the way.
We followed her past the old Dairy and Durante's' trailer park,
but while descending an embankment, a dog began to bark.
This hill – made up of rocks and clay with boulders scattered free,
is where my horse decided to dance right along with me.
Once again I held tight to what mattered and managed to stay in my seat,
but I'll tell you, I was never so happy as when I finally got back on my feet.
Next we went to Saltel's stables out on Alcona Road,
took turns going round the driveway – our joy was on overload.
We had a blast 'til the dogs ran the show; Justine went on her last ride,
she almost ate the doorframe 'cause the horse didn't slow when it went inside.
The last I went riding was near the foothills when out in B.C.,
but this time both horse and rider just enjoyed the scenery.
One day I will take lessons instead of just pulling on reins,
perhaps I'll gain some confidence – replacing the fear within my veins.

Human Nature

Human nature is so complex
it takes a little while,
to get to know a person
and their particular style.

Some are very selfish;
spoiled and cold inside,
others are happy and loving
and some have too much pride.

There are those who are shy and quiet
while others are ruled by greed,
and some will do almost anything
in order to succeed.

Some you will find are arrogant,
obnoxious and down right rude,
others can be abusive
depending on their mood.

Some are very special,
well adjusted and down to earth,
bringing joy and laughter
since the moment of their birth.

Personalities born to them
so different and unique,
add that to life experience
and the person is complete.

I Dreamt

I dreamt of you
before I knew
that you were on your way,
in dreams you seemed
to beckon me
to come to you and play.
At other times
we'd sit to unwind
I'd hold you on my lap,
you'd coo and smile
all the while
before you'd take a nap.
These many dreams
were real - it seemed
they played with my emotions,
to have another
again be a mother
was fast becoming a notion.
For when I'd wake
I'd hesitate
my dream had come to an end,
I'd feel alone
lost a comfort I'd known
depression became my best friend.
Then I heard the news
right out of the blue
you were two months on your way,
my dreams – they ceased
I felt at peace
and do to this very day.
For you my treasure
give me great pleasure
grand-parenting is the thing,
I can kiss, cuddle and hold
watch you grow 'til I'm old
happy memories you do bring.

Impatience

Impatience pays
a hefty price,
for it rarely seeks
common sense advice.
It pushes forward
creating havoc for fun,
grief is a given
before it's even begun.
With a mind of its own
and no thought to regret,
it continues through life
playing 'Russian Roulette'.
A very strong force
when left on its own,
instead of being 'nipped-in-the-bud'
while living at home.
Discipline hurts
on both sides of the strap,
but it's better than creating
a handicap.
For down the road
without discipline,
attitude thrives
always having to win.
Making it hard for friendships
to forge or survive,
'cause trust is diminished
as willfulness strives.
Impatience pays
a hefty price,
when no thought is given
before throwing the dice.

In a World

In a world of silence colors are bright,
detail and action are absorbed by the sight.
In a world of blindness, sound guides the soul,
a life lived on the inside – a sixth sense takes control.
In a world of living without the use of a limb,
obstacles are beaten with pride in a grin.
In a world of those challenged in any way, shape or form,
take life as it comes like the wind in a storm.
Achieving their focus – aiming high against odds,
dreams become reality where stands great applaud.
Bravely they master the will and the way,
that allows them to function a bit better each day.
In a world of those living with all function of being,
many speed through their lives without hearing or seeing.
Abusing their bodies, their health or their souls,
time travelled on empty with no ambitions or goals.
For some – belief in abilities and belief in themselves,
has been boxed up and hidden inside on a shelf.
This needs to be opened, let go and released,
to get on with their lives and try to find peace.
Stand proud of your person one-hundred percent,
you're a unique individual and perhaps 'Heaven sent'.
No matter the challenge, the obstacle or distress,
we're all in this together to learn and progress.
Laugh at misfortunes, malfunctions and strife,
all happens for a reason in all walks of life.
We're growing and learning at a pace all our own,
along the way do be thankful for any kindnesses shown.
Different strokes for different folks – all paths lead to one,
were here for a reason and a wee bit of fun.

Inspiration

At some point in time
throughout your lifetime span,
you'll meet up with a person
be it a woman or a man.

They'll inspire you onward
to much greater heights,
believing in abilities
you thought out of sight.

In turn if you're lucky
and if what you do - you do well,
perhaps you'll inspire
another to excel.

We're all here as teachers
and students to learn,
passing on information
along life's many turns.

We never stop searching
from a time in our youth,
about life and creation
or looking for truth,

Inspired

Inspired – this land
holds me tight
in its grip.

I work day and night
'til the sun
slowly slips.

Beyond the horizon
leaving shadows
behind.

The tools of labour
now too hard
to find.

I really must surrender
Father Times'
dimmed the lights.

I'll work faster tomorrow
while the sun
is still bright.

Kimmewin

You were a special
mother and wife,
a comfort to many
as you travelled through life.

Your heartfelt concern
for others you knew,
and everyday 'Greetings'
that brought smiles through and through.

Your cheerful disposition
on life as a whole,
the enjoyment you got
as you reached every goal.

Your yard work, the garden,
flowers and hedge,
strong determination
gave you the edge.

You loved the outdoors,
the water and trees,
now out at Kimmewin
your spirit can roam free.

We won't say goodbye,
farewell or adieu,
for you'll always be with us
in all that we do.

You were a special
mother and wife,
– our love will be with you
for the rest of our lives.

Live you're Life

We each live life as we see fit
not succumbing to total surrender,
for if we did it would never quit
for control knows either gender.

Man or woman; child or friend
they come in all forms and relations,
remember we're equal, a common blend
one of the good Lords creations.

Don't let temper, guilt or fear
make you feel so inclined,
to do another's bidding
at least not all of the time.

There's a bit of growing up to do
for maturity has no age,
but sometime in this life-time through
their lessons will be learned centre stage.

When they're a little bit older
and wisdom allows for new goals,
perhaps inaction will contemplate
'what's good for their body and soul.'

Just live your life as you see fit
helping out every now and again,
but don't let control take over
or ambitions will go down the drain.

Love is the Answer

Love connects
our hearts and souls,
to communicate with
or to console.
Someone with whom
to spend our lives
to lift us up
with inner drive.
To share our secrets
to share our dreams,
to hold and be held
in high esteem.
To walk together
hand in hand,
and feel secure
wherever we stand.
Love your brother
love your friend,
love your neighbor
and the world will mend.
It's there in the Bible
God's message to all,
love is the answer
to man's downfall.
To give of ourselves
as HE does from above,
that magical feeling
that's known as Love.

Love's Partner

Love finds a partner
in a woman or a man,
two souls connect
as they walk hand in hand.
An eruption of feelings
so strong in their wake,
bring senses together
as the mind takes a break.

Hearts beat a bit faster
with a rhythm of their own,
footsteps seem lighter
'Cloud Nines' their new home.
From the depth of inner being
a connection's been made,
this partner's your soul-mate
for life's escapades.

By the time that your thoughts
catch up to take lead,
hook, line and sinker
have been swallowed with ease.
'Cause loves found a partner
in a woman or man,
two souls have connected
as they walk hand in hand.

Macramé

I loved to macramé right from the start,
easily creating with a freedom for art.
A friend showed me a few of her true and tried tricks,
all else with enthusiasm was absorbed rather quick.
I bought a few books and continued to knot,
and over the years new lessons were taught.
It was useful for the hanging of fruit, flowers or soap,
curtains and holders made of wool or fine rope.
I liked to design – using materials on hand,
and couldn't wait to get started once thoughts had a plan.
I made a back for the piano as there was none,
a deer appeared out of nowhere – knots made one by one.
Hangers for mirrors, walls and door frames,
a spider and web to hanging over the windowpane.
The cord, beads and rings that I'd constantly use,
were near to impossible to find here in Sioux.
Roli quickly showed me how to macramé chairs,
so I searched high and low for those needing repair.
I've done lawn chairs and loungers and long table lamps,
until fingers, toes and back all had awkward cramps.
A curtain for the window of the 'Mack Truck',
with holders that held things without getting stuck.
It kept paper and hand towels up off the floor,
thus ensuring these items wouldn't roll out the door.
I taught classes at the Friendship Center on King,
and the girls were more than willing to try anything.
Creating from patterns or an idea in mind,
they showed a lot of talent and a knack for design.
The tying of knots and securing it to the last,
focuses your mind as you start to relax.
For while creating there's a form of release,
as a calmness takes over and your soul finds peace.

Me, Myself and I

Me – is very important it's the house
that forms the home,
for self-esteem and confidence
both need
a place to roam.
I – have got it together though Ego
rears its heels,
pride and greed
and selfishness
all try to make a deal.
Myself – has formed a partnership that's based on
mutual ground,
including me
and I of course
if reasons to be found.
Now me, myself and I rely
on honesty, trust and respect,
for that too
is important
or there's much room for regret.
Once I and We become a force
that synchronize with time,
life and love
will seem to flow
towards this heart of mine.
Yes, we've got it
together
Me, Myself and I,
we are the very
soul you see
when you look into my eyes.

Mind Reader

I'm not a mind reader, who sees into your thoughts,
whether you want to believe it or not.

And I can't tell the future the present or past,
all I can tell you is life goes by fast.

I do get premonitions, dreams and events,
heard voices at times that I know were Heaven sent.

Certain interests when thought of – draw knowledge to the door,
and like a magnet attracts books, Mentors and more.

Awesome things have happened though I can't explain why,
I just follow my instincts as truth verifies.

A voice or a feeling with all senses alert,
an earthly awareness that goes forward or helps you divert.

We are unique in our structure honing all human skill,
made in God's image though we're a mystery still.

I'm just an ordinary person an everyday soul,
trying to fulfil some of life's many goals.

To be heard, you must speak of what's on your mind,
or your inner most feelings will get left behind.

Enjoy every moment of each passing day,
don't dwell on frustrations or you'll wither away.

I'm not a mind reader but I listen real well,
so try speaking up and we'll sit for a spell.

Mr. Bones

Sitting in a circle
boards upon our laps,
our subject was a skeleton
who was very much relaxed.

As he hung there loosely
from a metal pole,
we focused on single sections
not upon the whole.

Four sketches were accomplished
in short periods of time,
using Jiffy markers
that filled the air like pine.

Next, we did full sketches
three of them in all,
sitting in different locations
with backs against the wall.

These were done in pencil
giving nostrils a bit of a rest,
hand and eye coordination
eventually progressed.

Mr. Bones came alive on paper
as we shared a chuckle or two,
another project finished
while exchanging points of view.

My Feet and I

I played with my toes in my very first year,
they balanced my being when walking was feared.

Afterwards they took me for runs through the field,
cuts and blisters were cared for and then quickly healed.

They peddled me up and around our long street,
from there I continued to abuse my poor feet.

Running on cinders and gravel and prickly weeds,
taking me wherever the mind tended to lead.

Later I skipped and jumped from high things,
climbed, kicked and danced whenever we'd sing.

Working long hours – operating the gears,
feet going steady to shift or brake if not clear.

They've taken me for walks and held up pretty good,
yet I focus on my hands not my feet where I should.

I've never paid attention to this abuse and neglect,
until I watched my daughter pamper and perfect.

Shaping and filing with such care and intent,
a good amount of attention to each foot was lent.

Perhaps I'll go soak and massage my poor feet,
then trim, file and clear coat my nails for a treat.

After all they deserve it; they've carried me for miles,
and when I think of where we've been – I sit back and smile.

Natures Own

The first few years of enjoying this house
by the lake on Moosehorn Road,
ravens and woodpeckers flew all around
while mosquitoes shared my zip-code.

There were a few mice and squirrels
and of course the odd cat or dog,
I've even had snakes and chipmunks
along with families of toads and frogs.

There have been at least nine or ten partridge
a fox and at one time a bear,
a lynx that came with it's owner
and two skunks with nary a care.

In the last few years I've been lucky
introduced to a new kind of peace,
humming birds, ducks and a groundhog
and of course the Canada Geese.

I love to watch them fly over
in control of their pattern of flight,
but once they land – they tend to pollute
and if scared, they've been known to bite.

They also eat all the tender roots
that are buried deep in the ground,
killing off the chance for a garden
not much survives once they've been around.

I love this place overlooking the lake
as it calms all nerves and senses,
wilderness and Natures way
heals a soul without added expenses.

Odd Jobs at Goldlund Mine

When lay offs came towards the end
before they completely shut down,
I helped out in the workshop
building ladders for underground.
I also worked in the new garage
painting became my new skill,
the carpenters would just get finished
and I'd be behind them with brush and pail.
Next I was trained on the underground hoist
sending the elevator up and down,
I must have jerked a few miners
'cause my turn soon came around.
I think we went down six levels
before the elevator finally stopped,
I observed my ladders in tunnels
and myself inside of a rock.
We entered a large round hole
with water running down the walls,
there was a mini railroad
this was how the ore was hauled.
I got to run the engine
following tracks 'til we heard a blast,
we waited a few short minutes
'til the dust settled down at last.
We watched a miner drilling
then hooked onto the carts of ore,
headed back towards the elevator
then got in and shut the door.
It was a great experience
though I prefer to stand on ground,
my hand became much steadier
while moving the elevator up and down.

Onwards

When Destiny, Fate and Spirit Guides
connect in some small way,
the path you're suppose to be taking
opens up without delay.

Work and interests run side by side
reaching out for much higher heights,
the mind – content to be alone
focuses on the project in sight.

At least that's how it seems to me
while delivering loads back to back,
I see a lot throughout the day
as memory sorts and tracks.

Where a certain rock lays waiting
or a tree, some moss or a shrub,
marigolds or fiddle-head ferns
true nature is cherished and loved.

In spare time I gather these treasures
collecting at times something more,
perhaps a piece of driftwood
as I continue to explore.

I'm grateful for given ideas
from someone much higher up,
visions deep within my mind
at times overfills my cup.

Unseen forces guide me
when energy's all but gone,
accomplishments behind me
while inspiration drives me on.

Our Parents

From birth to childhood, teen to adult,
you always stood by us
no matter our faults.
We woke you with illness with nightmares and dreams,
and tested your patience
with childhood schemes.

The going got tougher with each passing year,
but still you stood by us
so strong and so dear.
You both learned endurance, stamina and skill,
and managed to survive us
and our battle of wills.

We learned to respect you – our parents, our guides,
with a deep sense of love
and strong family pride.
Joan worked Security at the Dryden Mill,
and had her own business
and Artistic skill.

Dan continues to serve and work with the Police,
open and honest he loves
keeping the peace.
And then there's the Trucker – little old me,
who feels right at home with the rocks,
moss and trees.

We all thank the Lord for blessing us with you,
good-hearted people
who are honest and true.
You always stood by us no matter our faults,
from birth to childhood,
teen to adult.

Paper Girl

(Liz)

Introduced to the workforce early on in my teens,
by a gal who showed promise
and exhumed self-esteem.
She delivered the paper after school each day,
no matter the weather
it was never delayed.
I helped her fold papers on the hard cement floor,
in the basement of the Day Block
by the back entrance door.

I can still smell the ink mixed in with the dust,
and the odor of dampness
as eyes tried to adjust.
The room was dark and dingy with few lights overhead,
which threw many shadows
where the papers were spread.
We inserted the flyers then folded and packed,
took our leave in a hurry
to fulfill her contract.

I followed beside as we covered her route,
in the rain and the blizzard
wearing jackets and boots.
She was liked and respected for her nature and wit,
and years later I see
she still hasn't quit.
She's moved up in the workforce though still going strong,
with a smile on her face
she's right where she belongs.

Peace

When Ego
is put upon a shelf
- no longer
used to brag,
when everyone's
treated equal
and tongues
no longer wag.

When pride and anger
take 'Time Out'
and compassion
gets to rule,
when jealousy
and spite give up
and no longer
ridicule.

When all the hurtful
ways of man
are put to rest
at last,
and the 'Back
to Basic' lifestyle
is within
each persons grasp.

God's children
will emerge with grace
and love
all living things,
Peace will flow
throughout the land
as all the
Angels sing.

People Meet

People meet
like stars at night
and share their thoughts
and inner sights,
then part like eagles
in the sky
after having said
their last good-bye.

As time goes on
they're bound to meet
no longer strangers
on the street,
another friend
to pass the time
when days are long
and not so fine.

Or even in
the mornings light
a friend can start
your day off right,
and so like stars
that stand alone
people too are
on their own.

The eagle
soars to highest
peek,
the more friends
you have
the more
you will
meet.

Poems

*Poems seem to come
in flashes at times,
without concentration
they're focused in mind.*

*Sometimes these poems
are completed with ease,
as fingers dance quickly
across all the keys.*

*And then there are times
that I don't understand,
when words seem to flow
right through my hand.*

*These poems are finished
in no time at all,
the inks on the paper
before thoughts get involved.*

*Some come more slowly
just a glimpse of a thought,
they are quickly recorded
for time later sought.*

*Poems seem to come
in flashes at times,
with the play of the words
and the rhythm and rhyme.*

Quiet Moments

In my comfy old blue jeans and loose fitting shirt,
I'm happy and at home sitting down on the dirt.

My pulse seems to quiet; my blood pressure drops,
relaxed in mind and body all worry soon stops.

I file my thoughts allowing for peace,
quiet moments when chatter begins to decrease.

I ascend through the clouds that are fluffy and white,
colors soon take over within my minds inner sight.

A pale green brings calmness as relaxation flows,
then blue and purple that seem to sparkle and glow.

At times I see a meadow, both lush and alive,
where butterflies and humming birds have already arrived.

Down for some water then to the flowers in bloom,
my vision gets better for I find I have Zoom.

Sweet harmony just like the Good Lord has planned,
visions within the minds eye at command.

A golden hue follows and fills me with peace,
a time well remembered when stress levels peek.

Record in Time

I used to believe all was well with the world,
of course that was when I was just a wee girl.

As I grew older – 'twas like a slap in the face,
nothing had prepared me for the true human race.

Brought up in a home that taught right from wrong,
where manners and actions with conscience belonged.

All people equal – no matter race, size or gender,
without morals and ethics ever having to surrender.

But boy, once you leave the 'home nest' for good,
how well you had it – is then understood.

'Out in the world' can be a cold, lonely place,
challenging your nature with fears you must face.

So many individuals with different natures and traits,
jealousy, aggression, love, anger and hate.

Greed and destruction – the need to control,
what happened to peace and the love of all souls.

Crimes and convictions, loss of life due to war,
lets look for the beauty and let go of the horror.

Through the eyes of wisdom, let humanity shine,
our past – a vague memory – a record in time.

Together all people can live and repair,
what negative actions have destroyed without care.

Replenished & Revived

Pine trees grow from little corns,
into strong, tall trees 'til old and worn.

Especially when damaged by natures pests,
the woodpeckers, bugs and perhaps a Ravens nest.

Eventually the needles do turn brown,
and soon enough they're all over the ground.

Each time it rains the needles flow,
forming little clusters as moss does grow.

A cover for the forest to keep moisture in,
mankind can cause damage but Nature will win.

It may take a few years to cover our tracks,
to be dug up eventually as artifacts.

God's creation will continue to thrive,
for thousands of years it has replenished and revived.

It's really quite amazing to see this first hand,
a tree growing through steel or pavement– a strong force in the land.

I've seen them on rooftops or in a crevice on the cliff,
growing with character usually both strong and stiff.

Coliseums and castles have forests for floors,
both time and the elements have rotted windows and doors.

It makes one wonder what other treasures will be found,
for the earth tells no secrets as it holds you spell bound.

Scottish Pride

I've too much Scottish Pride inside
far more than my fair share,
it sure makes life ' hard living'
for I'm sensitively aware.
Each word to me that's spoken
each act or gesture seen,
I analyze with scrutiny
for the sake of my self-esteem.
Past experience with different aspects
that seemed to come along,
obstacles met and challenged
through the years have made me strong.
Lessons learned while on this journey
have made me cautious and aware,
taught me to understand people
now intuitions are treated with care.
My instincts have all been sharpened
and they say wisdom comes with age,
so I sit here patiently waiting
for this knowledge to be fully engaged.
My English side encourages
much time spent on my own,
my energy levels much higher
when amongst my rocks and stones.
Goals are always set too high
but stubborn tendencies strive to win,
I seldom want to call it a night
for I've lights I can always plug in.
I have everything I need right here
rocks, gravel, sand and clay,
a wheelbarrow, rake and shovel
and lots of room to dig and play.
Ambition comes from both my folks
many lessons were learned by their side,
hard work was never shirked by them
they stood by their morals, ethics and pride.

Self-Belief

All it takes is one person to confirm self-beliefs,
about life and its wonders no matter how brief.

For when the mind gently opens and is inspired to think,
thoughts focus inward connecting the links.

Imagination is kindled as possibilities grow,
there's so much more to this world than we'll ever know.

Who's to say what you're thinking is your thought alone,
perhaps to millions of people this fact is well known.

When something spectacular is witnessed or felt,
don't feel alone – many hands have been dealt.

You aren't the first and you won't be the last,
minorities are formed as the ignorant laugh.

Unwise to the workings deep in their minds,
still looking for the answers you've already defined.

Different levels are travelled at a more comfortable pace,
content with the knowledge they've thus far embraced.

Others need to touch, to feel and see,
they haven't the Faith to let their minds to roam free.

Inwards and upwards or down with Intent,
to meet animal Totems or Guides Heaven sent.

This takes a bit of practice and most sessions are brief,
all it takes is one person to confirm self-beliefs.

Shadow

Where'd that shadow come from
that walks beside my life,
I see it in the sunshine
and also late at night.
It somehow keeps me company
as I continue on my path,
I wonder what its thinking
when I talk, or sing or laugh.
It carries all the baggage
life lent on a loan,
while learning earthly lessons
and fighting the unknown.
Fears, failures, and rejection
grief, sorrow and pain,
repressed for the most part
except when down Memory's Lane.
It's probably best forgotten
as time travels on,
else how could one function
from daylight 'til dawn.
A clear mind and conscience
for discussions debate,
new thoughts and new memories
to accumulate.
I know not where it comes from
nor where it goes when it's gone,
but I appreciate the presence
of this phenomenon.
It cleans the brains data-base
and helps tow the line,
allowing me more memory
and of course – more peace of mind.

Sioux Lookout

Sioux Lookout has been my home
my choice of a vacation place,
why would I want to go anywhere else
when there's so much here to embrace.
The trees, the shrubs, the underbrush
the moss and berries for free,
not to mention the rocks surrounding us
so much beauty for the eye to see.

Many beaches to relax on
to run and play or swim,
all you need is time for yourself
so your senses can take it all in.
A variety of flowers surround many homes
along pathways, gardens and yards,
incredible landscapes – well cared for through time
show the results of outstanding regard.

Most of the people are friendly
good-natured and down to earth,
but of course there are those as in every town
who ensure appreciation of the first.
There's something here for everyone
in our little town of Sioux,
sports and recreation
for those with excessive energy to use.

There's also a beautiful golf course
and a riding centre at Cedar Bay,
a Roy Lanes or Robins coffee
to help start or finish your day.
So why would I want to go anywhere else
when here's where I love to be,
there's less strain on the wallet
and I can travel now on net or T.V.

Sixteen

*Achievement brings
such a feeling of pride,
for you and the parents
who've stood by your side.
Teachers who've guided
and nurtured your mind,
friends who are treasured
as one of a kind.
And now that the age
of 16 has arrived,
the future awaits
as you learn how to drive.
'G1' and 'G2'
bring no guarantees,
for you must meet requirements
to retain a 'G'.
Obey all the rules
the signals, the stops,
avoid speeding for it quickly
introduces the Cops.
Once you've mastered all skills
and are licensed to drive,
the responsibility is yours
to ensure you arrive.
So that later when alcohol
tickles your nose,
you'll surrender your keys
as you wiggle your toes.
And likewise when catching
a ride with a bud,
your life's in their hands
so "What's in their Blood?"
Live life to the fullest
for there are many rewards,
many years of excitement
and much to explore.
You are a treasure
to many fine folks,
so to yourself be a Hero
and live to tell jokes.*

So Happy Inside

I love to wake up early and sit myself outside,
with a cup of tea or coffee
– I'm so happy inside.
I capture dreams on a clipboard pretty much every night,
then rewrite them in the morning
with pictures on sight.
I color in the objects practicing all lessons learned,
this way they stay in memory
– images quickly return.
Little stories seem to gather throughout a period of time,
depending on thoughts and actions
I've had on my mind.
For when dreaming the subconscious gives us a role,
and for the most part we have courage,
strength and control.
At the time things seem real – so life like and true,
adventures and journeys
where gravity's unglued.
I've floated to the moon and then back to earth,
in the seventeenth century – poor clothing showed worth.
Ears popped each time the ozone was passed,
the Universe was awesome with it's all STAR cast.
Other times I've floated a foot off the ground,
without effort I moved
wherever thought had me bound.
Yes, I love all my mornings; it's a great way to wake up,
before going inside
for my second cup.

Spiritual Being

Each soul has knowledge and ability
though consciousness interferes,
that and societies preaching
and decades of not thinking clear.

What happened before the churches
before people were burned at the stake,
for visions and premonitions
God given senses for goodness sakes.

Like sheep the people followed
out of fear, not from belief,
gifts lost for more than five hundred years
are returning piece by piece.

For those who are open minded
to universal energy, life and love,
'a giving and taking of power'
is what the whole world is made up of.

Each of us is a psychic being
within both mind and soul,
we each have premonitions
for our senses make us whole.

If you'd spend some time in silence
exploring your inner mind,
I think you'd be very much at ease
and surprised at what you might find.

Intuition has saved me a few times
through bad thoughts, vibrations and dreams,
understanding it all takes longer
'cause I'm just a simple Spiritual Being.

Spirituality and Religion

Our physical beings rely on support,
a place of true worship for groups of all sorts.

That's where religion comes into play,
people can kneel together and pray.
Feel a brotherly love and kinship to all,
hear comforting words within the church walls.
The energy transmitted in a group such as this,
gives a boost to your being – a sense of pure bliss.
The worship of God - no matter culture or race,
is a nurturing, caring and peaceful state.

Spirituality is something you do on your own,
going within and seeing how much you've grown.
Lessons you've learned and those you've ignored,
pathways you've chosen and the memories stored.
Negative thoughts and actions released,
for they only bring hardships discomfort or grief.
It requires analyzing thoughts on both life and goals,
every issue you've faced and those you behold.

Facing up to bad Karma and dealing with depts,
bad attitudes and judgments and personal regrets.
By opening yourself to the love you deserve,
energy will flow and touch every nerve.
It will give you a boost - charge up your system,
by sending it within and then outward with wisdom.
Spirituality and Religion go hand in hand,
God's light is within every woman and man.

Every child created is a part of this light,
and it's right there to guide us when our souls take flight.

Stress Levels

Automated phone services
create much of life's stress,
taking time to get an answer
to a question you want to address.
"Press one" or "press two"
or "stay on the line",
'cause you're one of many
who are waiting for a sign.

Music plays in the background
as the voice mentions all deals,
and of course all the ads
that to some might appeal.

Every now and again
the voice brings you news,
on how close you are getting
to their sales service crew.
No wonder stress levels
'due to technology',
are higher than normal
due to lack of employee's.

Automated phone services
make some sigh in despair,
you know you're there for awhile
so curl up on the chair.

"Are the offices empty?"
or "On coffee break all day?",
or are they on strike
wanting more pay?
My time is important
I've better things to do,
than patiently wait
on the phone to get through.

Strike Out

(1980's)

We called ourselves the Expose'- our colours were red, white and black,
we had our gloves all ready as we left the home team shack.

Ian and Tim were the coaches and we appreciated their point of view,
giving their free time to coach us into a batting and ball catching crew.

There was our Back-Catcher Diller or else Terri Lynn,
guarding home plate as the runners came in.

Carol and Shirley were pitchers no doubt,
when they struck out a player you could hear our team shout.

Laura-lee and Shirley both covered First-Base,
waiting for the action that was about to take place.

For Barbara and Sandy it was Second-Base they shared,
they tagged a lot of players as the dust filled the air.

Joan's place was Third and she protected it well,
to get past her they had to excel.

Suzanne was our Short Stop usually catching those flies,
with that and her Chattering she kept Team Spirits high.

Linda, Liz and Kathy were ready one and all,
out in the field as the Batter hit the ball.

Laurie, Bobby and myself in the Second Half went in,
and if by chance we caught one – we would surely grin.

Wesley's was our hero, Score-Keeping was his claim,
always busy marking runs we'd make throughout the game.

Supply and Demand

What is life
but lessons and learning,
feelings and emotions
as the world keeps turning.
Many lives it might take
to get everything right,
then back to the Heavens
where Spirits unite.

Once in our Soul Groups
we energize Self,
analyzing our lifetimes
and personal wealth.
Children we had
and held for awhile,
pathways from birth
all neatly compiled.
Did we accomplish ambitions
or must we return,
to strive for more goals
with more lessons to learn?

This is debated
deep in the mind,
but in the end it will come
I'm sure you will find.
For we're made in Gods image
and united we stand,
pure light and energy
meet supply and demand.

Sweet Innocence

Child of the Universe
exhuming such light,
as you come forth
your spirit's so bright.

Energy and wisdom
so close to home,
now out in the world
with thoughts of your own.

Exploring and touching
and receiving such love,
sweet innocence surrenders
to those standing above.

As you grow forward
each on your path,
memories are recorded
on an invisible graph.

Attitudes and opinions
patterns, habits and ways,
personalities and traits
you've collected each day.

Far away from beginnings
and the wisdom of birth,
decisions in life are now
made here on earth.

Taxidermy

I took an evening course one year
so I could tan some hides,
I found it very interesting
for we had an experienced guide.

I wanted to learn about rabbits
but worked on a bear rug instead,
carefully removing all the fat
using scissors to trim body and head.

The skull lay on the table
as I finished the rest of the hide,
then after being cured and brushed
felt was sewn to the underside.

The head was attached to form and felt
the teeth, tongue, and eyes remained,
the face – built up with putty and pins
was painted and then it was stained.

I mounted some birds and tried a few fish
though the latter turned to mush in my hands,
much the same as the porcupine
though I saved the quills for future plans.

I also mounted a rack on a plaque
which hung by the bar in McFees,
wrapped with moose hide instead of felt
the hunter was very much pleased.

I enjoyed learning about this special art
it's an interesting and skillful trade,
preserving the animals structure and grace
techniques that are very well paid.

The Bagpipes

The sound of the Bagpipes
captures
my Soul,
for whenever I hear them
they make me
feel whole.
From the time I was a young
and all through
my teens,
when the Pipers' were Piping
I was watching
the screen.
No interruptions
I blocked
them all out,
my father understood
without
question or doubt.
For later in life
he confided
one day,
that the Bagpipes affected him
in much the
same way.
It's like an inner haunting
that penetrates
the Soul,
as the Pipers' would pipe
and continue
to stroll.

The Fairy Flag

Many centuries ago on the Isle of Skye,
comes a legend of love that has somehow survived.
The handsome Laird of Dunvegan, sought by many it's said,
fell in love with a Fairy whom he wanted to Wed.
The King of the 'Shining Folk' at first refused their request,
as broken hearts would soon follow the two being blessed.
For the Chief was a mortal and would soon age and die,
the Fairy Princess – heartbroken, had tears in her eyes.
He agreed to 'Hand-fast' them for a year and a day,
if she returned to them freely with no earthly array.
Happiness followed the Princess and Chief,
they soon had a son though it filled her with grief.
For the year and a day in a heartbeat were gone,
the King and his Fairie Raide in all finery shone.
At the end of the causeway they sat down to wait,
as promised – she followed with no thought to escape.
Lady MacLeod hugged her child then laid him to rest,
gained a promise from her husband that their son would be blessed.
He'd never be lonely or have reason to cry,
for she couldn't bare the anguish of him being denied.
She ran from the Tower and joined her people, her folk,
to the 'Land of the Fairies' on fine wisps of smoke.
Laird MacLeod remained alone and in depressed state,
the loss of his Lady left him mourning his fate.
On his Birthday a feast was put on by the Clan;
agreeing he danced to the Piper's demand.
The Maid left in charge of the precious wee lad,
went to see the festivities and the colorful plaids.
So enraptured she didn't hear the babe when he cried,
and in an instant his mother was right by his side.
Magical Words were then whispered which he'd later recall,
before wrapping him up in the famous "Fairy Shawl".
It was a talisman that was left to protect the Macleod's,
in dire need – three waves of the flag were allowed.
It was waved in 1490 then again in 90 years,
for a Battle and a Cattle Plague as starvation was feared.
In the Tower at Dunvegan the delicate 'Fairy Flag' awaits,
the next plight of the Macleod's at the free hand of fate.
A myth or night story to be told to the young,
or a Legend in the heart of life's songs to be sung.

The Games of our Youth

The games of our youth are etched deeply in mind,
each day a new adventure was ours to find.
No cobwebs were formed from us sitting around,
for we ran and we jumped and played all day long.
Imaginations ran wild and so did our feet,
as we travelled up and down our own private street.
Government Row was a paradise right here in Sioux,
we were fortunate to live in the place where we grew.
Playing house or dress-up with table and chairs,
riding on backsides all the way down the stairs.
Marbles and Hopscotch, Jacks and Double-Dutch,
or digging with spoons to fill pots, pans and such.
Barbie's and cut-outs were our favorite event,
much time cutting dresses out of catalogues was spent.
Knock on Ginger was popular as was Hide and Seek,
both kept us moving and quickly so to speak.
Hula Hoop and Bike-Riding or Exploring at will,
coloring and drawing or playing King of the hill.
There was Hockey and Football or Baseball for fun,
and of course enough children for two teams on the run.
Kick the Can and Dodge Ball or a game of Horseshoes,
friends seemed to gather right out of the blue.
Tag and rock-collecting or building roads for Dan's cars,
and listening to my sister as she played her Guitar.
A canoe and a rowboat that were built by my dad,
were ours for the taking – we didn't have it so bad.
And like fish born to water – we swam everyday,
built forts in the summer to keep boredom at bay.
Imaginations ran wild and so did our feet,
as we travelled up and down our own private street.

The Good Lord

I love the good LORD and I love my life,
though I've had my share of personal strife.
He created much beauty on this blessed earth,
we've treasures to enjoy of such wholesome worth.
A feast for the eyes and creative mind,
ideas and inspirations that are easy to find.
Relaxation for the body on either land or lake,
a calming for the soul when taking a break.
Each tree, each shrub, each blade of grass,
His spectacular vision had a touch of class.
The moss and the flowers, the rocks, water and sky,
not to mention the clouds that continue on by.
The Aurora Borealis, sunset and sunrise,
the moon and the rainbows, the stars in the sky.
The birds and the animals to natures delight,
run, climb and play or if able – take flight.
So much to mankind has been given to use,
though money and power have destroyed and abused.
Greed, pride and ego take a stand to justify,
dishonoring the earth with an eye for an eye.
Murder, war and destruction go hand in hand,
little value on life or for the law of the land.
The results are astounding, take a look around,
with ozone depletion – harmful rays hit the ground.
The earths own protection shredded and torn,
an unstable future to which we've been warned.
Waste products are buried in Mother Nature's womb,
instead of separating the components initially exhumed.
If there isn't a way – these products shouldn't be used,
more research is needed before action's pursued.
Going green is the answer and giving back to the earth,
for this Kingdom is ours and it has a great worth.
It's an inheritance to our children and on down the line,
haven't we had enough warnings or acknowledged the signs.

If we continue on track we'll derail in time,
and if we don't put our foot down then we're partners in crime.
We each have to try and do our own part,
and though it may be too late we need a jump start.
As of yet where I live it is quiet and serene,
many tourists come to visit for beauty and cuisine.
Fresh water fishing and boating on a holiday whim,
brings them to Canada time and again.
Yes, I love the good LORD and I love my life,
and I know I'm responsible for any successes or strife.
Willpower and freedom gave me that choice,
and like many I have a conscience and with it a voice.

The Light Within

The light is within you
please let it shine,
as you ask for protection
and open your mind.
Relax all your body parts
focus with intent,
find your true purpose
in the silence that's lent.
You may see some colors
you may see a form,
if this is the case
then you're getting warm.
Your third eye will open
if given the time,
it's like traveling upwards
towards the Divine.
Soft clouds all around
as you ascend,
meet up with your Angels
they are your best friends.
From the day you were born
they guide and protect,
but as we get older
we tend to neglect.
Life gets so busy
the silence fills with noise,
prayers ease the conscience
but vision is destroyed.
To reconnect with our being
you need only go within,
there in the silence
where life ends and begins.

The Missing Kayak

I clearly remember my time in grade two,
we each had a project that we needed to do.

We'd studied the Eskimos; how they lived, what they ate,
so while I worked on my essay, dad started to create.

He fashioned a kayak out of birch bark and glue,
by down-sizing the pattern from his homemade canoe.

Then out of his pile of discarded wood,
he carved a two-sided paddle the best that he could.

Working hour after hour well into the night,
to surprise me in morning when it came into sight.

I was thrilled and excited that he'd taken the time,
I was so proud of my father and his homemade design.

I enjoyed it for an hour before handing it in,
then sat down and waited for the class to begin.

Weeks after, all projects were returned with a mark,
but mine had 'just vanished' was the teachers remark.

No questions were asked, no mystery solved,
which made me suspect that my teacher was involved.

Intuition has told me over the years,
that it sits on a shelf perhaps in front of a mirror.

For I've thought long and hard and still wonder why,
she didn't question, didn't look, didn't rectify.

In her care and supervision she held all the cards,
she had the power and control, but lost my regard.

For decades this has shattered my faith in man-kind,
for trust has been an issue in the back of my mind.

My fathers love and efforts leave a pain in my heart,
for I remember the kayak as a great piece of art.

The Monarch Butterflies

June fifteenth of ninety-six
days after mom passed over,
I went to Umphreville Park for awhile
and sat amongst the rocks and clover.
A Monarch butterfly circled me
five times before flying away,
I sat and wrote from memory
things my mother used to say.

As I readied myself to leave this place
the butterfly repeated the same,
five times it went around me
then back from where it came.
A few days later I returned
to jot some more memories down,
this time two of them approached
and again went five times around.
Then again while I was packing up
they repeated this ritual once more,
five times they seemed to go around
and my energy started to soar.

It was a sign from the 'Heavens"
for these were a favorite of Moms,
now sure she was with my Nana
my grief dissolved into crumbs.
For 'Heaven' is our true home
once lessons are learned here on earth,
I now follow all signs and signals
putting all knowledge to verse.

The Raven's Nest

The birds are so busy building their nest,
I love sitting to watch, as I take a short rest.

They're amazingly smart – professionals at hand,
with big branches in beaks they're still able to land.

Some of these twigs looked about four feet long,
without too much effort they were placed to belong.

If his mate was having trouble or was taking her time,
he'd let go of his branch and to the skies he would climb.

He'd fly in a big circle with style and class,
check out her progress and squawk as he'd pass.

Then land in a tree not too far from his objective,
the branches kept falling as he was very selective.

Seemed as soon as his mate flew away for awhile,
he got into perfecting the nest with great style.

Over time, it grew in both height and in size,
from the ground you'd only see them, if they decided to rise.

They finished long before the cold winter set in,
the gathering of supplies was well disciplined.

I watched them all winter while throwing out scraps,
at first they were cautious - well prepared for a trap.

But now when they see me they check out `our' spot,
to see if the landing is worth what I've brought.

The Storm

Across the lake the rain did pour,
lightning and thunder cracked and roared.
The wind picked up and clouds rolled in,
hair stood on the tops of goose bumps and skin.
The waves in their force doubled with caps,
trees bent just as far as the flexible sap.
A couple were twisted right off their trunks,
leaving few branches on what remained of a stump.
Howling, the wind echoed as more shadows appeared,
the clouds were now darkened evoking raw fear.
The tip of the lightning near touched the lake,
as rain drops quickly hardened into hail in its wake.
Like pellets each rain ball drove down with such force,
leaving much damage as it danced its main course.
Roadways, soon rivers, moved boulder's and sand,
construction would be costly due to washouts and dams.
The saturated ground held onto footsteps and prints,
soggy and slushy, the frogs swam in short spurts.
Birds hovered in nests above and beyond,
once all had passed over, there remained a few ponds.
Squirrels and chipmunks held fast in their holes,
well-stocked for the winter, they hid out like moles.
No cats or dogs were heard above the howl,
of the wind and the rain as the thunder roared and growled.
Then a big crack made my heart jump and skip,
looking for cover as lightning continued to rip.
Like jagged fingers – arcs covered the sky,
then all settled down and seemed to pass by.
A few clouds here and there, as a rainbow shone bright,
the calm after the storm was a beautiful sight.
It stretched from frog rapids well into the trees,
so long and drawn out the camera's eye couldn't see.
But three prints later I was able to get the full scene,
A panorama snapshot would have sure reigned supreme.
It was quite exciting, emotions ran wild,
maturities instincts bring you back to the child.
Especially when alone with trees sixty feet high,
I tend to hover on panic, feet ready to fly.

The Voice

You meet a new friend who seems awesome and cool,
but may have hidden agenda's
with you playing the fool.

This is when life's lessons should be called into play,
contemplating the outcomes
of actions underway.

Think of your parents and all those you know,
will this make them proud
or will your cheeks start to glow.

Friends are a great comfort for passing the time,
as long as fun doesn't turn
into committing a crime.

The voice that guides you gently comes from within,
and the wisdom it shares
is called discipline.

Go with your first instincts they're always correct,
and when following them
you'll find self-respect.

Be your own person – unique in your being,
true to yourself
and in all of your dealings.

Therapy

When prescribed it implies 'more pain in store',
or so I first thought as I walked through the door.
I was put in a cubicle and told to lie down,
so I took off my shoes and put on a gown.
I was a bit nervous – my muscles were tight,
I imagined the worst and was ready for flight.
Then Yolanda arrived to access all my pain,
a simple case of whiplash she went on to explain.
Starting with a heat pack wrapped round my poor neck,
muscles were knotted I felt like a wreck.
She proceeded with Ultrasound to penetrate deep,
showed me some stretches that I'd have to repeat.
Then with my limp head secure in her hands,
she'd pull, twist and turn – I was hers to command.
One particular stretch had me facing the sky,
she said "wiggle your nose" but I couldn't comply.
I wasn't a rabbit but I gave it my best,
my face was contorted lips tightly compressed.
Well she started to laugh once she saw my mistake,
she meant move my head not my nose for Lords sake.
Each time I went back I felt more at ease,
the girls were cheerful as they'd joke, laugh and tease.
Next was my back – seems it popped out of place,
my tailbone and hip bone no longer touched base.
But in no time at all with a few tricks up her sleeve,
the pain in my back was greatly relieved.
A few tired muscles but with stretches and time,
thanks be to therapy I soon felt just fine.
I've learned to respect this Medical Field,
for without it our fates would surely be sealed.
These human 'Pain Killers' have wisdom beyond years,
their knowledge and know how work wonders it appears.
I can walk without clicking, work all day without pain,
I've gained a new lease on life without going insane.
I appreciate the time and care I was given,
and for the relief that allows enjoyment of livin'.

Time Waits for no Man

Time travels fast as it drags us along,
though perhaps we're not ready
or don't feel we belong.
When young we wanted action and patience wore thin,
all was in the future
and we couldn't wait to begin.
Thirteen was the age limit to babysit for cash,
a quarter for housework
or taking out the trash.
We couldn't date 'til fifteen but we could venture the matinee,
ride our bikes home much later
as the story was replayed.
A learner's license at sixteen to drive your parent's car,
eighteen for some shows
or to party at Bars.
All seemed to take patience for safety's own sake,
but once all was accomplished
we wanted to brake.
For when younger – time travelled so terribly slow,
but then it sped up
as we watched our kids grow.
Now 'Freedom Fifty-five' is looming ahead,
and Retirement round the corner
as we hold tight to the thread.
Time waits for no man as it tick-tocks away,
our perception is clearer
then it was yesterday.
Always rushing through life to grow up and move on,
if only we knew
we were right where we belonged.

Time Well Spent

At times I have the feeling
that you stand by my side,
counter-acting my reactions
making me smile instead of cry.
I get a flash of your face
smiling, happy and content,
and am comforted by the knowledge
that our time was well spent.

So many good memories
you left in our care,
and when given a moment
I often go there.
Back to the time when
when I was just a small girl,
on Government Row
'in our own little world'.

Home-made root beer and popsicles
swimming morning 'til night,
a canoe and a rowboat
at our disposal on sight.
Making forts, riding bikes,
collecting feathers and rocks,
or the times you'd hang laundry
and we'd sit and just talk.

Those few summer nights
when all ready for bed,
we'd be off for mile 7
to watch the bear cubs instead.
Time traveled too quickly
without us being aware,
the future – now past
like a wisp of fresh air.

To Every Child

To every child
be true
to yourself,
love one another
and
everyone else.

Be kind
to your neighbors
your family and friends,
like a flower
that naturally
dances and bends.

For when
hearts are happy
and conscience is clear,
there is nothing
to run from
and nothing to fear.

Absorb
your surroundings
with happiness of soul,
all things
that you learn
will in turn make you whole.

Spread your
fine wings
as intelligence grows,
a positive
energy
to cherish and know.

Two Worlds Entwined

Earthly spirits pass us by
knowledge then is magnified,
energy levels begin to excel
as elements align and get personal.
Nature surrounds us
nurturing our souls,
spirit guides us onward
to much higher goals.
When concept and understanding
open new books,
thoughts and intuitions
are given second looks.
When closed doors are opened
they too will then see,
unwritten but experienced
by simple folk like me.
I've had premonitions
and dreams that came true,
experiences with butterflies
and flowers that grew.
Been led to some rocks
with messages from above,
for our Lord and my parents
I have a great love.
I'm very open-minded
needing neither proof nor print,
I talk from my experience
of separate incidents.
Believe or disbelieve me
it really matters naught,
for I have all the evidence
with each and every rock.
So keep your senses open
to the Universal Mind,
both Worlds are connected
to all that is Divine.
I leave no room for skeptics
perhaps speaking out of line,
but all experiences – I believe
because of course they're mine.

UFO

(Early 80's)

Like a Good Year Blimp it hovered over the pines,
lights flashing underneath which brought focus to mind.

It travelled the same speed as we travelled by truck,
and to tell you the truth we were kind of awe struck.

For about five to ten minutes I looked to the sky,
and for once in my life I was completely tongue-tied.

It was dark in the fall at about six o'clock at night,
then with the snap of two fingers – it was gone out of sight.

We travelled the North Road in silence and thought,
then all at once we were talking for the answers we sought.

The two fellows' with me admitted they'd seen it too,
but also said they'd deny it for sanity's point of view.

My mind raced with excitement in what I had seen,
as we followed the highway and the headlights bright beam.

About twenty-five minutes later we topped the last hill,
which joined onto Alcona when I felt that last thrill.

There it was hovering at the end of the road,
as if waiting for our arrival – the lights continued to glow.

It stayed a few moments before it was gone out of sight,
it travelled an L-shape – taking off to the right.

It would have passed over town within the blink of an eye,
and once again I felt blessed for looking up to the sky.

The Radar Base apparently picked it up on their screen,
and it arrived in Vancouver three minutes later it seems.

I can still see it clearly when I focus in thought,
and ever since I've looked upwards more often than not.

You never know what you'll see or what visions are in store,
for the world is a wonder – there's much to explore.

Weather Controls

The weather controls accomplishments
determining ambition and drive,
depending on inspiration
and deadlines that often arrive.

The sun fills us full of raw energy
but can be draining if too hot or dry,
at times it's better to put off for tomorrow
the work that would slowly drag by.

When the rain and winds combine their force
and ground becomes muddy and rough,
it makes it hard to keep up your pace
though for me that just isn't enough.

I've got rain suits and rubber boots,
and gloves that don't seem to leak,
and I find goals on these cooler days
much easier to complete.

It really doesn't matter
once `drive' takes over control,
strong thoughts and pure ambition
seem to motivate this old soul.

Imagination and focus
helps to keep me on track,
as well as `sense of humor'
when taking a step or two back.

There's always something to do
in the rain, the sun or the snow,
as long as there's ambition
and the get up to go.

Wise Words

'Do as I say
and not as I do',
words of great wisdom
so often are true.

Habits embraced
are habits well learned,
and habits are something
not easy to spurn.

So 'do as I say
and not as I do'
is advice from those caring
about what happens to you.

If your looking for habits
and a bit of a high,
challenge ambitions
and reach for the sky.

Allow your true Spirit
to shine it's own light,
respect your fine body
by showing foresight.

To be wise while youth
has you fast in it's grip,
is one step ahead
of those giving you lip.

Words

No thought to what comes out of our mouths,
when upset or angry at who, what, or how.
Like a double-edged sword we weld such a power,
that ten-fold comes back as a karmic shower.
Words, thoughts and feelings that we carry in vain,
filled with negativity like an acid rain.
Do hit the target but also return,
we get what we give as we live and we learn.
Calm your frustrations and lower all stress,
love what you do and give it your best.
For that is your reason for being alive,
it's what feeds your ambition, your passion, and drive.
Whether it's artwork or music; a book or a poem,
a skill or a craft or creating at home.
It's a part of your being – a part of your soul,
learn to laugh at misfortunes and show you're in control.
No one else matters when dealing with fate,
as Karmic dept is paid off and you have a clean slate.
Live life and be good to neighbors and friends,
make sure words and actions don't hurt or offend.
When mad - bite your tongue and then count to ten,
or else say a prayer and let it go with 'Amen'.
For it takes a big person to ponder and weigh,
when attacked or accused or rubbed the wrong way.
Your health will improve, relationships too,
when you watch what you think, what you say and you do.

Writing in the Rain

As I patiently wait
for the rainfall to quit,
I pick up my pen
and I write as I sit.
I finish, I edit,
and I start poems anew,
depending on what my brainwaves
lead me to pursue.
Could be the weather
or a place that I've been,
objects of nature
or people I've seen.
A known place of business,
an adventure or friends,
a news event, an opinion,
or new style or trend.
Whatever memory
my mind focuses on,
verses are compiled
and some pictures are drawn.
I love to write poetry
it's forever on my mind,
and it's the best way I know of
to help a soul unwind.
Releasing thoughts to paper
with pencil or pen,
if not often – then at least
every now and again.
I find I feel better
– not all bottled within,
thoughts are out in the open
with a few drafts in the bin...

Yesterdays are Forever

Yesterdays are forever
they never let go,
inner visions and memories
have total control.
Thoughts appear out of nowhere
a face flashes by,
the past like a shadow
never bids you good-bye.
A time and place is remembered
enjoyed and relived,
perhaps slights and wrong doings
allow one to forgive.
For the most part growth and knowledge
soften our hearts,
we know right and wrong
don't walk too far apart.
There's a very thin line
between actions debate,
life and death, peace and war
and of course love and hate.
As human's we experience
upheavals and shifts,
and it depends on our natures
whether we stand or we drift.
Therefore a positive outlook
ensures a chuckle or two,
less stress in your life
and good memories too.
So when you do have those flashbacks
you can feel satisfied,
about the past and it's shadows
for they never bid you good-bye.

Your Basic Palette

Your basic palette creates many shades,
mixing and matching
for whatever's portrayed.
Some use Cadmium Red or Crimson instead,
but it really doesn't matter
just so long as you have Red.
Then Cobalt Blue or Ultramarine – it's really up to you,
but in order to paint most anything
you pretty much need a Blue.
Cadmium Yellow or Lemon add light and it is calm and mellow,
so be sure to add a little blob
of the color that's known as Yellow.
Raw Amber and Burnt Sienna or else Yellow Ochre hands-down,
this really is a must you see
for it's the color of Brown.
To Darken a color add a bit of black to the primary hue for shade,
start with just a little
until it makes the grade.
To lighten a color just add some white to the primary for tints,
a little goes a pretty long way
so take this as a hint.
For Warmer colors to cozy up add Yellow to the color you choose,
but if you want it a bit Cooler
just add a touch of Blue.
Primary colors are blue, yellow and red – mixing will make many more,
so get yourself a Palette
and have fun while you explore.

About the Author

Sandy was born and raised in Northern Ontario and throughout her life has written poetry as a way of expressing her inner thoughts and emotions. She has met many interesting people on her path and feels blessed by her many friendships. Her career choices have always been demanding, but also very fulfilling. As a heavy equipment operator/ truck driver for 25 years, her world expanded taking her to other towns surrounding the Sioux Lookout area. A love for nature and the outdoors has inspired many of her poems, as have the people, places and happenings around her. Sandy has a remarkable way with words and the rhythm of her poems is soothing to the soul.

J.H.